Raising Well Learners

Helping Parents Support Students
from Stress to Success

Deena Kara Shaffer, PhD

Author of the best-selling "Feel-Good Learning: On how to
prioritise, focus, study and learn everything better."

For more information and permissions contact:

Pandamonium Publishing House

Pandapublishing8@gmail.com

Printed in Canada

Published by Pandamonium Publishing House
Publishing Made Simple.
www.pandamoniumpublishing.com

Book design by: Pandamonium Publishing House

Cover design by: Pandamonium Publishing House and Haily Appel

ISBN Paperback: 978-1-998467-04-4

First Edition: October 2024

Praise for Raising Well Learners

"Our students aren't thriving, and we need to stop settling for that. Raising Well Learners flips the script and puts students where they belong—right at the center of the Venn diagram of wellness and learning. This book calls out outdated approaches and offers a fresh, holistic strategy that sees students as the whole, incredible humans they are. It's all about fostering real academic growth while making sure their emotional well-being is front and center, not an afterthought."

- Vanessa Vakharia, Author of Math Therapy™: 5 Steps to Help Your Students Overcome Math Trauma and Build a Better Relationship With Math

"Deena Shaffer's Raising Well Learners is an invaluable resource for parents and educators alike. With palpable compassion on every page, this guide offers practical and effective strategies to enhance students' academic performance, emotional well-being, and social skills. It's a must-read for anyone dedicated to fostering holistic growth in learners."

- Saundra Yancy McGuire, Ph.D., author of best-selling books Teach Students How to Learn and Teach Yourself How to Learn
Director Emerita, Center for Academic Success and (Ret) Assistant Vice Chancellor, Louisiana State University

"In this inspiring book Deena Kara Shaffer offers a holistic, comprehensive approach to working with learners by placing a value not only on academic pursuits but also on the value of relationships, belonging, contemplative practices, family, community and the natural world. This is the book parents and educators have been waiting for."

- Laura I. Rendón, author of Sentipensante (Sensing/Thinking) Pedagogy. Educating for Wholeness, Social Justice and Liberation

"Raising Well Learners offers kind, insightful, and empathetic guidance. It's packed with practical strategies for parents and caregivers to help students manage time, gain focus, work better in groups, and increase motivation—all while lowering frustration and chaos. This is the missing handbook to support your child's learning."

- Avery Swartz, founder & CEO of Camp Tech and best-selling author of See You on the Internet

Table of Contents

Introduction

Being a Well Learner

Being a well learner means doing and feeling okay in school and life. It's not about being perfect, but about having the skills and support to deal with challenges.

To be a well learner means making awake, aware, intentional efforts in schoolwork. This involves seeking feedback that aligns with those efforts, rather than spending inefficient hours on a project or studying that winds up in a dismal grade.

It's *not* about straight A's, or a particular GPA average, but rather feeling motivated, engaged, and in healthy relationship with stress.

To be a well learner is to have a sense of connection and belonging.

It's *not* about having an extraordinary teacher, reliable group of friends, or formal mentor, but rather feeling welcome and valued in learning spaces.

It's *not* about chronic sleeplessness, exhaustion, or burnout, nor is it about skipping or avoiding.

Being a well learner involves prioritising holistic health and well-being, rather than solely focusing on academic success.

To be a well learner means having the ability to make it to morning classes more often than not, if that's part of the semester's schedule.

It's *not* about unwavering focus, but rather maintaining clear-headedness and concentration during important moments, such as lessons or lectures, and having the skill to reclaim attention when it wanes.

It *is* about learners recognising their role in their own learning journey, feeling connected to supportive networks, being encouraged and welcomed to voice their thoughts and ideas, embracing their identities, and finding comfort and care within the school community.

It *is* about learners feeling more in balance and equilibrium—that their school, work, volunteer, community, social, and inner lives are all being tended to here and there.

It *is* about learners reclaiming some of their time for more rest, play, or joy.

It *is* about learners knowing what to do when their teacher or professor assigns a task or project, instead of stewing, avoiding, procrastinating, panicking, or putting the project or instructor down.

It *is* about learners knowing how to engage with studying effectively: knowing when to start and when to take breaks, and efficiently preparing for exams by mastering remembering and recall techniques.

It *is* about learners knowing how to restore their focus, even if only a little, through holistic, health-promoting ways.

I'm not suggesting all of these. And I'm certainly not suggesting all of these *all* the time.

I want every learner to feel represented in this book, and every parent and family member to feel welcome. I am acutely aware of just how much can get in the way of any of these aspirations. I don't want *not being shown how* to be one of them.

You might be wondering, "Why aren't schools teaching this stuff?" While schools should ideally provide supportive environments for learning, sometimes they fall short. My life's work and passion lie in addressing these shortcomings—when students feel pressured, judged, shamed, forced out, or excluded instead of encouraged to thrive.

I'm in the deeply beloved vocation-based work of "then what?" I'm not prepared to say "no" to a learner who wants to learn. Instead, I offer a myriad of things to try.

If a system's processes and priorities are getting in the way, I'm not one to sit idly by. I refuse to wait for change when students are in need. While I actively work to dismantle and disrupt barriers, my lifelong commitment is to provide solutions for students who seek alternatives and strive for a different experience in school.

It's about learning strategies.

I'm the biggest fan.

If I said, "they're great, but they're not the end all and be all," I'd be hiding my enthusiasm. If I said, "they're remarkable, but they're no panacea," I'd be masking not just my passion, but my research *and* most importantly my experience beside countless students who have transformed their school lives and beyond.

I had a supervisor once who really detested the word "transformative." He thought it was overstating things. He thought it was hyperbolic. He thought it was arrogant.

And yet.

If a student is shown *how* to learn, they *can* learn. Their potential knows no bounds and they can achieve far beyond what they thought possible. They can regain health, they can access more of what's being taught, they can participate more fully, they can feel their confidence grow, they can earn marks that open up things like grad school or internships or scholarships.

Learning has a ripple effect, touching every aspect of a student's life. Without understanding how to navigate the educational system—which is at the core of learning strategies—students may find themselves held back or even pushed out. This can lead to feelings of shame and a tendency to hide their struggles.

Learning strategies are, for me, stunning in their potential. They're where mental health and well-being, equity and access, and academic performance all come together.

Learning strategies are the blueprint of *how* to do school. And how to do it while feeling and staying well at the same time.

Sharing learning strategies with families is at the heart of raising well learners. Not just physically well or emotionally and psychologically well or spiritually well—but also *academically* well. That learning feels possible, doable, and sustainable.

The work of well learning

I'm a marketer's nightmare. (And I don't see that changing.)

I've had pinpointed advice to focus on one "thing,"on one "group" of people.

But!

The work of well-learning belongs to us all. It's not only educators who hold this. And it's not just students themselves. It's for all those in and around a learner's life. And learning strategies are the key.

Learning strategies aren't one thing—they are about productivity, yes, and they're also about mental health, coping, equity, joy, accessibility, pedagogy, belonging, and performance.

And, learning strategies are for students. All of them. Every year. Every subject. Every experience.

And, learning strategies are for educators. Across the disciplines. They make teaching better.

And, learning strategies are for parents! They're every bit as frontline as teachers are.

But!

To be clear, I really mean many more folks than parents. I'm talking about and welcoming in *all* the people involved in raising learners including parents, extended families, chosen family members, siblings, mentors, athletic coaches, spiritual supports, loving neighbors, and community members. There can be a diverse network of individuals supporting a learner's schooling and development journey.

There can be a number of people along for the ride in a learner's schooling and development. And I want them—*you*—to feel all the way included. This is written for you.

This is written to exclude as few as possible.

This is written with warmth, kindness, and an invitation for all.

If your learner has dyslexia, dysgraphia, dyscalculia, cerebral palsy, sensory-related disabilities, acquired brain injuries—these and other important lived experiences will need additional ways of tending. That doesn't mean you won't find supportive strategies here. But specific interventions are likely useful.

Likewise, if your learner is struggling with significant anxiety, severe depression, borderline, or suicidality, this can be a friend to you, but not the only one. Trusted mental health professionals will be helpful, and I encourage you to seek out resonant, representative support.

Raising well learners

To raise a well learner is to nudge.

It's to encourage, invite, model, mirror, and nudge again.

And what's *in* that encouragement? What's the *content* of that nudge? Learning strategies.

Without being explored, demonstrated, or reflected upon, the transformative potential of learning strategies remains untapped.

When modelled—when nudged—*that's* where there's opportunity for alchemy.

Learning strategies aren't just capable of changing lives; they actively do so *when* learners are exposed to them. But there's a disconnect: few people are aware of these strategies, they're seldom taught, and learners have limited opportunities *to* learn about them.

I've had students weep with relief upon being introduced to them. Some have transformed from failing to achieving Dean's list status, while teachers have expressed gratitude and relief in discovering them, eager to integrate them into their pedagogy. I've even heard of school principals encountering learning strategies with absolute shock, having never heard of them before.

And then, of course, there are parents and chosen families. What about them?

If students are *seldom* taught, parents are *never* taught learning strategies.

Most parent education has to do with school *behaviour* and discipline, getting kids to help out around the house and whether or not to incentivise this, how to communicate with teens, how to support them through bullying, how to get them care for anxiety. But nothing that I've come across teaches parents to support their kids in *how to learn*.

Learning strategies are my jam, my passion, and my professional dedication. They're what I research and write about, they're what I coach and keynote on, they're what I love learning more about. They've been the thread through all my roles, and in all I publish.

So, what are learning strategies? And why would these two words, boring-ish when put together, mean so much to me, and the thousands of students I've worked with over the years?

Because they change everything.

If you teach a learner how to manage their time, they get more of it to live their lives fully, engage in more of what they care about, and feel less stressed.

If you teach a learner how to move through homework and assignments with less resistance and more awareness, they do better, sleep better, and there are fewer family conflicts.

If you teach a learner how to study efficiently and effectively, their confidence and marks begin to soar.

If you teach a learner how to prioritise their time, tasks, and their passions, their panic goes down while their productivity goes up.

If you teach a learner how to write well, especially if they've never been taught or feel like they can't do it well, then their identity as a student shifts, and more possibilities for the future open up.

When a learner feels good about and in their schoolwork, they do better; when they do better, their well-being improves; when they do better, family harmony amplifies; when they do better, the next thing opens up, whether that's post-secondary, grad school, or professional opportunities.

For me, learning strategies are not just an academic intervention, but an equity, accessibility, and health one too.

Through learning strategies, more learners are included. More learners have a voice in a classroom. More learners feel welcome, resourced, and capable.

It's no wonder why I'm so passionate about ensuring that parents and families, in all their diverse forms, are also familiar with learning strategies. When parents understand these strategies, they can seed-plant, suggest, and slip them in when their kids are struggling. Parents can do more than get frustrated, sit beside them to pull the work out of them, or suggest that they "go talk to their teacher."

In every learning strategy lecture I teach, I always—I mean 100% of the time—hear, "I wish I knew these before!" or "why didn't anyone teach us this?" That's what led me to start sharing with *parents*. Now, I offer learning strategy *parent* circles—low cost, all families welcome, fill-your-pockets-with-strategies group sessions. And I'm keen to share them with you.

Now, let's discuss how to approach conversations with your kids about learning strategies. There are learning strategies, and then there's *talking* to kids about them.

Parents can start by being straightforward and saying something like, "here's a suggestion I picked up that might help."

Parents can hand over this book, or my earlier bestseller, "Feel Good Learning: On how to prioritise, focus, study, and learn everything better,"and have them read a passage, chapter, or the whole text.

Parents can *do* the strategies with the learner as a kind of duo or group project of sorts—how to be more productive, for example, with less of a cost, physically, emotionally, and spiritually.

Parents can casually have this book lying around, ready to be glanced at by your learner when no one's around.

Parents can subtly hint at the beginnings of an idea, moving towards it bit by bit, without offering a specific technique outright—like musing over burn out without whipping out a new agenda for your learner to try.

Parents can try learning strategies themselves and share what's working—*without* recommending it to learners, and letting it hover.

Parents can try learning strategies and clearly share how these are so helpful! "You should try this!"

Parents can *not* try learning strategies and talk about their experiences, what's hard in their work world in terms of planning or prioritisation or remembering or focusing and consider aloud what you *might* try.

Parents can try learning strategies all together as a family and reflect regularly.

Parents can make a kind request of their learner to try one or two.

The critical elements are to communicate clearly to learners that:

- Learning strategies help make things easier.
- Learning strategies help lighten the cognitive, and emotional, load.
- Learning strategies make comprehension, confidence, and marks go up.
- Learning strategies make stress, worry, and fatigue go down.
- Learning strategies aren't about doing *more* school.
- Learning strategies are about doing school *more* efficiently (to ultimately have more hours to do *non*-school things).
- And that it's not their fault that they didn't know—no one taught these to them before!

It's also important for me to make clear to you, and for you to make clear with your learners, that strategies take the place of shame of judgment. And sometimes, which is the goal here, these hacks and rethinks become lifelines—and professional tools for their work lives in time.

What to prioritise in sharing this work with your kiddos?

- There are times of openness, and times of *really* closedness.
- It's more worthwhile and more fruitful to seed-plant over solve.
- Listening may be the most helpful tool you have—sometimes your learner isn't seeking a solution or recommendation, but a kind ear, safe place to vent, or to let the pressure valve release from the day or semester.

And when your learners *do* try learning strategies, there will still be bad marks here and there, there will be mistakes made, hurdles encountered, disengagement in some contexts, and flubbed assessments. The great thing is that these can be so crucial to learning.

Above all else, and more important than any learning strategy, is the importance of relationships. The bond, the connection, the deep trust you have built and continue to nourish with your learner. This is more important than acing a test, or than a strategy being heard or tried. If your learner is shut-down or closed off, then the priority becomes being a compassionate, supportive presence. It becomes being a soft-edged, co-regulating source of reliable care. When your learner comes back online, *then* try again.

Above all, what I want for you to take away from *Raising Well Learners*, is that underneath the content that learners might be struggling with, is an opportunity to radically and elegantly reconsider the *how*.

PART ONE

GETTING TO IT—HOW TO GET YOUR KIDS TO START THINGS (AND FINISH THEM)

As parents, we can feel so helpless when we see our kids floundering in their homework, "wasting" their time, struggling to get things done.

And that helplessness can come out as fatiguing frustration, as sharp barbs, as a pulling-out-one's-hair feeling.

We can't do the work for them, even though it might seem doable, simple, easy, and quick for us to blast through.

We can't tell them outright what to do—we all know how that will land.

We often wind up telling them what they're not doing right—that the phone is a distraction, there are too many tabs open, starting too late, and leaving things until the last minute. And, again, we *know* that well that goes. Which is to say not at all.

Luckily, we can swap out helplessness for sharing the "how" of planning and organising with our kids.

You *might* be initially met with closed ears or even closed hearts. Or you might not. Lightening the load for your learner by way of time management and prioritisation learning strategies comes with relief much more often than resistance, both in the moment, and in the form of long-lasting skills.

After that initial raised eyebrow, or straight up eyeroll, learners can hear that time management frees up their time, eases their workload, and makes life easier.

You may try a workaround—like saying, "you know, I came across this time management technique that gives you so much more time to hang out with your friends...wait, nah, you've probably got some good procrastination strategies."

You've honoured your learner's agency *and* let them know that there are ways for them to feel less stress and more success, *and* that you know some.

More often than not, your learner will ask you to clarify, ask to find out more, and soften that closedness or resistance. It might not be immediate, but we're talking about seed-planting.

Helping your kids get to it—whatever that "it" is, from starting that studying to starting that essay to starting that lab to starting that problem set to *finishing* it—is something that we can help with.

It might need tact, it might need a light touch, but strategies to get to and through the work can surprisingly be something they seek out and take your two cents on.

Chapter 1

Relating to Time

Does it feel for your learner (and maybe for you too) like there's never enough time to do all they (and you) need to do?

Does it feel for your learner (and maybe for you too) like there's a quality of always-rushing, just-making it, barely making deadlines?

Does it feel for your learner (and maybe for you too) like time's always running out?

Does it feel for your learner (and maybe for you too) like there's not enough "free" or leisure time, or that most (or all) of the day-to-day is work?

Regardless of the simplicity or complexity of the schoolwork ahead, time always seems to be in short supply for students. It's a constant struggle, a relentless tussle, and often feels like an all-out battle with time.

In this chapter, we'll explore supporting learners in their relationship with time—how to utilise it more efficiently and effectively to tackle the tasks at hand (the work we *have* to do), while also freeing up time for the activities they enjoy (the things we *want* to do).

Time management as the big opening chapter is intentional. It's usually the first session with clients, the first lecture in my university learning and well-being courses, and the first thing learners of all ages ask me about.

Sometimes, it's in the form of scheduling—like a desire to make a study schedule when exam season nears, or how to "fit" stuff in, like school deadlines alongside sports tournaments or varsity games and family commitments and part-time jobs.

Sometimes, it's in the form of balance-related wonderings—like wanting to feel more spaciousness in the day-to-day, having better quality sleep, and how to spend more time with loved ones.

Whatever the specific words or iterations, students across the ages and years *always* ask me about time management.

The first thing I do is ask them about their *relationship* to time: Does it seem to disappear in an instant? Does it always seem rushed or frenzied? Does it float by? Does it cause punishing worry?

Why this question? And, why "relationship?"

Because we can't *manage* time. It's not a bossable, controllable, containable thing.

We can change our relationship to it—we can shift how we plan, we can rethink the number of tasks we take on—but we can't change *time*.

I spend time wondering what another phrase would be other than time management. There are specific techniques, like time-boxing. There are poetic ways of putting things, like time yielding. There are poignant descriptions that get to our deepest existential worries, like time-anxiety. And there are workarounds, like *capacity* management.

Yet, the phrasing "time management" persists. So, for lack of better wording *for now*, and for ease, I'll use this too. But what I'm really talking about is how to get stuff done within a timeframe.

Getting stuff done in a timeframe is tough, for just about everyone, and it seems like no matter the app, it *stays* tough. I read a wonderful article not long ago, and the title alone brought a smile to my face—it was something to the effect of, *Time Management Can't Be Solved with an App.* That's not it exactly, but it's the gist.

There are so many things to buy, so many patented things to try, so many analog or digital tools to deep dive—to procrastinate *with*—and yet isn't it remarkable that despite the variations, despite all the options, time management is so hard for so many?

In this chapter, I'm going to do some small throwdowns. There's a lot to cover, and in the spirit of time management, I'm going to make each short and sweet.

Kind counsel

The starting place with your learner on all things time, tasks, and that tight feeling of *never enough*, or rushing, or being late (or almost late) *again*, is to normalise it.

It is hard to get stuff done. It's especially hard when there's lots of "stuff." It's *especially* hard when those deadlines collide, like a test and project and presentation all clustered around the same day or two.

The first sigh of relief can come for your learner if you share your own time management struggles. Do *you* procrastinate—on what types of tasks? *Doing* what? Do you know why?

I'm not suggesting you make your struggles theirs, but rather to name either what it was like when you were a student if you had similar experiences with stressful time crunches, or if you ever feel that way now.

Relating, laying bare what's broadly hard, and reassuring the normalness—that *almost everyone struggles with this* or *everyone feels like this*—goes a long way. After all, to feel alone and ashamed *on top* of feeling short on and stressed for time makes things worse.

Your learner is most certainly *not* the only one struggling in their relationship to time, and I'm a big fan of sharing just how hard and human it is.

The real lesson

If only *all* learners could understand and take comfort in the fact that managing projects, devising timelines, pacing work over time, prioritising tasks amidst pressing demands, and meeting deadlines are just as much work as the content is.

Teachers don't often reveal that, if ever. And it's not directly on a rubric or marking scheme. Yet it's just as much a part of an assignment or assessment as remembering information, solving problems, or crafting a lab or paper.

Figuring out the how—the process, the stages, the steps—is as crucial as the product.

I've heard it phrased as something like honouring the outputs—the daily chipping away, the clear-seeing and efforts along the way—more than the outcome or product—that final project submission.

What would happen if you phrased it like that to your learner?

That "managing time" was actually 50% of the project. It's not going to get a checkmark or a numerical grade but is baked into the assignment.

They *might* write you off. At first. But a seed would be planted. You're revealing a hidden element that *is* very much part of what's assessed.

After all, there *are* late marks for things—often 10% a day deducted for a submission handed in after a due date. To hand something in on *time* has an implicit demand for having thought through and met milestones to get there.

And while your learner might say that they could whip off a paper in one evening and the teacher would never know, you can let *them* know, from me, a teacher, that they know. Time management shows up in the quality of work.

Relating to time is the real lesson, and I encourage you to name that for your learner.

What's being borrowed

The thing to look out for from your learner is what they're borrowing from.

What do I mean?

In their struggles with time, are they borrowing from their sleep? This happens *a lot*. We take minutes, or even hours, from our sleeping time to keep working on an essay or problem set. Yet, borrowed sleep ricochets, and always loops back around for us. It happens in the form of getting sick—then we lose even more time. It happens in the form of fogginess, sluggishness, and exhaustion—making listening to a lesson or lecture, or moving through a school workload, even harder and slower. It happens in the form of burnout—putting at risk the capacity to persist through a course or term. We'll go into sleep much further on, but for now, one way to tell whether concern is warranted is if your learner is pushing the edges of appropriate bedtimes later and later.

Or are they borrowing from family life? If reaching deadlines is causing your learner to skip family meals and events, more than once in a while, then there's a relationship-to-time issue that's worth helping your learner to explore. Fam jam time can happen, it can be protected and participated in; your learner needs to be shown how. That's what we'll do momentarily. But for now, help them see that borrowing family time is helpful feedback for rethinking approaches to time management.

Or are they borrowing from friend life? Isolation and loneliness are now headlines, and even referred to in pandemic language, because of how potent their impact is on quality-of-life markers. Interestingly, they also affect things like GPA. Shutting out the world and zeroing in solely on work might be okay once or twice in a year for a massive project just before a submission, performance, or launch date. But doing so regularly is a flag for support around time-relationship.

Or are they borrowing from their physical health? We're now deeply aware of the consequences of prolonged sitting, screen hunching, lack of movement, and shallow breathing. It is my strongest opinion that the goal post for success has moved. It's no longer success at all costs, but *sustainable* success. Success that doesn't come at the expense of physical well-being. If walks, team sports, exercise, or movement of any kind keep getting triaged out because of workload, there's another invitation to have an important conversation, and deep reconsideration, of how time is feeling and going for your learner.

Context matters

Time is hard to relate to *not* because of your learner. *Not* because there's anything wrong with them. *Not* because their outlook, their approach, their ways of being are "problems" that need "solving."

Instead, time is hard because of the context we live in.

There are oppositional pressures and societal structures and stuck systems, all of which make it *seem* like the problem is the individual student, but this is flawed.

Let's take the very devices that most learners have in their pockets or on their desks as you read this sentence. They are *designed* to be riveting and irresistible.

The society we live in is one of hyper-consumption—always more to buy, so then there's more work that needs to be done to afford it.

Think of the words currently being associated with work right now: grind and hustle. I'm *all* for hard work, but I'm worried about pervasive toxic productivity. That we're grinding away at our work (talk about a joyless, machine-based word), or hustling (trying to do a little over here, a little over there, moving things around, and with honesty at risk).

I don't have rose-coloured glasses on. I don't think learner life, or professional life, can be all flowers and sunshine. But I *do* think we can call out the way that intense go-go-go is structural and not an innate flaw in our kids.

Yes, our learners can benefit profoundly from learning the skills of scheduling, prioritising, planning, organisation, and project management. Yes, our learners must understand what they personally do to move through their work *and* honour health, and social and family connections. Yes, our learners need tools to push against distractedness (I offer many in this book).

I want to ensure we're not *blaming* our kids for it being so hard. Each of them, each of us, faces an onslaught of sensory input, wildly entertaining gadgetry, genuinely competing priorities, and deadlines.

This isn't a fault issue, it's a humanity one. In the meantime, let's work through supports that can help ease the time-pressures.

What's underneath

Back to that article title, *Time Management Can't Be Solved with an App*—what's it getting at? There are scores of apps, websites, and physical planners.

There are systems, acronyms, "methods," checklists, inventories for time, and trackers.

There are tools and tricks aplenty. But unless what's *underneath* them is left unexplored, there can't be much insight or realisation, and therefore not much shift or transformation.

So, what *is* underneath. I'm not going to fake-rank this in order, I'm not going to constrain it into alliteration. Challenges with time management include:

Not getting enough sleep and physical exhaustion. The question becomes, what's interfering with a good night's sleep? Is it erratic bedtimes, worry at night, not enough sunlight or physical movement during the day, or not enough pleasure sprinkled throughout? There's that bedtime procrastination phenomenon of staying up for pleasure even though it comes with a cost the next day. As a starting place with your learner, prioritise sleep well-being so that they can have their full faculties to think and talk about time and planning in a clear-headed way.

Not knowing where to start. This is seldom taught to learners. When you get a project, you know the deadline, but how on Earth do you *get* there? I'll share specific strategies in a moment, but whatever the process, *ask* your learner how *they* intend, envision, or plan to move from the assigned date to the end date? Due dates don't reveal the process to arrive there, and that's an enormous learning curve for students. After they share their approach (or lack of one), share yours—how *you* get from A to B, whether something is due in a week, month, or longer.

Not recognising what gets in the way. While there's a lot of judgment, harsh words, and frustration thrown at learners, steps before this can be conversations about the hurdles and roadblocks they face. Is it distraction? Or, is it relational, like interactions with "friends" that lead to high drama, conflict, and rumination, impinging on focus and energy to do homework? Is it around struggles to focus? Moving a learner's workstation, investing in noise-cancelling headphones, having a no-phone box outside their room, or using a social media blocking app could be supportive micro-interventions.

Not being honest about what's happening. A missed or skipped class can lead to a second and a third, resulting in a learner having no idea what to do, what the instructions are, where to begin, or what the information or content is all about. This can lead to layers of shame piled on top. It can be almost impossible for a learner to say to their parents or chosen family, "I don't actually understand what's going on." Gentle check-ins like, "that looks like a tough assignment, what's it all about?" or "what are you being asked to do for that?" can be helpful for gauging your learner's comprehension. Innocuous but purposeful questions can help you gain access in a different way rather than, "do you not understand what to do?" Keeping distance from further shaming, benign and strategic questions that plumb what's *really* going on for your learner can help you find your way in.

Help them get to know what's *really* happening for them in their relationship with time. Then, the app, method, or tracker will have a purpose, and be likelier to stick.

Counting backwards

One of the best approaches to planning is to teach your learner counting backwards.

I share this with humility. I wasn't originally going to write about this as I thought, perhaps, *maybe* it was obvious. That you'd roll your eyes. And then, wouldn't you know, I got a big wake-up call and now am fully committed to including this strategy.

Just a few days before writing this section, during a coaching session with a student, this was precisely the strategy we used. They're a first-year science student in a competitive program who received top marks in high school. They are working with me due to the common transition shock experienced when moving from secondary school to university. They now realise, in their own words, that they, "got away with procrastination in high school because there was so much less to do." They have experienced a 20% drop in marks, and their mom reached out to me.

We started the session with a "word of the week," and they said, "stress." They spoke it in a way that felt like it was more than usual. They shared feeling confused about where to start, and how to make headway, particularly in the end-of-term season when workload volume feels both amplified and compressed.

The way they expressed their confusion and uncertainty about "where to start" made me notice the opportunity to precisely discern that starting place.

Their to-dos were still floating. Even though all were due within a two-week period, weren't yet anchored to a schedule. So, we worked backwards.

- We listed all the due dates.
- We made note of all the lectures and other blocked time.
- We wrote out the no-go times—it was their birthday *and* there was a religious event their entire family was celebrating within that timeframe.
- We then listed the work in terms of components, and this is key! Instead of "study" or "read" or "review" or "prepare" or any other generic, unclear verb, we needed *specifics*. Like, how many practice questions to study each day, or how many pages or chapters need to be read.
- We broke each component down into doable, manageable chunks. For instance, they mentioned that they'd need to spend roughly 1.5 hours of reading. After some questioning, they reflected on being most alert when reading for no more than 30 minutes of dense material at a time. So, we were now able to factor three 30-minute reading sessions on this fleshed-out to-do-list.
- From there, we counted backwards: if this is due on this date, you have these available time windows, and the work needs to be done in this many sub-tasks or chunks. Where will they go?

The result felt miraculous to them!

It wasn't hypervigilant, it wasn't planning done in anxious 10-minute windows. Rather, it was clear times for clear tasks, all done by working backwards from the due dates.

It can feel messy, like when it's time to spring clean a closet, and everything gets pulled out first. But in doing that work-back plan together, by laying it all bare, by making it messy first with sub-tasks and chunks and blocked windows to honour commitments and life's joys, we could then assign actual work to actual times.

Clear windows

Part of what had made it so difficult for this student to know what to do and when was the lack of evidently clear windows. It was all a bit of a blur when they looked at their next two weeks.

Two popular time management strategies—time boxing and time blocking—only work when there are empty spaces in the calendar or when there are spaces that could be emptied, delegated, or shifted around.

Time boxing focuses on the time, while time blocking centres on the activity.

When a learner time boxes, they establish a box of time in which to do tasks. I prefer the image of a window (expansive) to a box (enclosed), but they're parallel. What stretches of time can your learner find in which to do work?

This seems obvious. And yet most students don't do this. Instead, they have an embodied knowing that a list of things must get done by a certain date—manifested in tightness in the chest, a gripping in the body, even sleeplessness—but they haven't set aside time for each of those to-dos. They overlook the windows—the time expanses they can box. Time boxing is great for multiple to-dos, like 30 minutes of reading, 10 practice questions, writing two paragraphs, all within a boxed off time window of an hour and a half.

When a learner time blocks, they designate an activity for a particular time. It entails not checking social media, avoiding distractions like browsing tabs or responding to emails and texts, and instead, immersing oneself deeply, focusing intently, and exerting energy in a directed manner without interruptions. This approach is effective for cognitively challenging work that becomes more difficult when fragmented, prolonged, or disrupted by switching between tasks. Time blocks are great for concentrating on a single task and maintaining a singular focus. This would be great if a student had 45 minutes and spent it on one lab or paper that requires research, idea development, or generating written content.

The key is to help your learner look at the reality of their days and weeks ahead and what windows of time they can see. From there, whether by box or block, they can assign tasks to time, instead of an etheric, anxious, "oh, it'll all get done" mindset.

Get agenda-ing

I never thought I'd spend so much of my professional life talking about agendas. I love it, I do it with delight, but it is with a little bit of surprise.

On one hand, there's the impression that learners are totally resistant to using things like an agenda. On the other hand, given their knack for finding the latest trends in almost every aspect, it's assumed they already know the newest organisation-focused apps.

Interestingly, I hear learners of all ages and years say, "I keep it all in my head." As in, all deadlines, and how to reach those deadlines, mentally.

I also hear those same learners say how stressed, overloaded, and burnt out they are.

That's when I introduce using an agenda.

Why does this always land so well? (And it does, in truth, *every* time.) It's because no one ever taught them how to use one, or it was just a thing that maybe one kid did in class, and it looked out of reach, weird, and something that *other* students used.

When they start using one themselves, everything changes.

Agendas can be transformative for many learners. They show up to our sessions each week *wanting* to show me how they're using their agenda—consistent, colour-coded for some, and organised.

How can an agenda be transformative?

Because it moves what's carried so heavily, erratically, with unpredictably in the mind onto paper or app. The mind has less to hold. Then, learners can see the *when*. What we've just been exploring—where those windows are for boxing or blocking. Learners can also see when they'll complete something—easing a restless mind before bed that worries, "let's just keep going tonight to get this done." It's not necessary, the learner can *see* when it'll get done—they've planned for it! Learners can also see where their breaks, fun stuff, and other commitments go. They can say a clearer "yes" and "no" to the things they have agency over.

With an agenda, learners can plan based on reality, not assumptions or memory lapses. Clear documentation eliminates guesswork and mental clutter. No more guessing, no more mental chaos, and much less worrying.

"Default" rethink (aka assume less)

With agenda in hand, with windows ever clearer, a great conversation to jump into with your learner is about what their "default" day or workload is.

At that, what's yours?

Mine is a bit too much, what about you? It's a life project for me, like so many, not to overfill my days.

The antidote is to rethink and re-architect what the default "setting" is on the day. As in, instead of, for a professional person, filling the 9-5 day *full*, having it be ⅔ to ¾ full.

Why?

So that there's room for: flexibility, tasks that take longer, collaborative conversations to pop up, bursts of creativity, feeling a bit under the weather and moving more slowly, or any number of unknowns.

Shifting that internal standard setting on how you and your learner fill your days allows for the realities of life—what we can't control. It makes space for variables and unpredictability.

It also moves away from that fine edge where everything is down to the wire.

I try to do this myself with just about every project. I do this by assuming I'll have fewer days than are actually there. I know that every *seemingly* available day won't turn out to be available. One of my kids will get sick and need my full presence. A work snafu will arise requiring time and emotional labour.

Just because I can count the days to get something done, doesn't mean I can *count* on them, or that I'll have full access to them. *This* is my starting place and is now my default.

Help your learner see that they might not have all the minutes and hours they initially assume the night before a project is due to work on it. Have them move that due date earlier. Help your learner see that they might not have quite as many days as it appears at first glance to study for that midterm two weeks from now.

Assume there'll be fewer minutes, fewer days, and all around less—time, energy, capacity—than it looks like. If they wind up with sweet, wind-at-their-back kind of days, weeks, or months, then what a boon! How lucky! They're finished early. If it's a regular time where any number of things get in the way, then they've planned for it.

Planning time for what can't be planned for!

Unclenching practise

The final offering I'd like to suggest around relating to time really centres the holistic approach of this book, and all my work. Namely, to bring in the body.

So much of time-bound work is done clenched. Clenched forehead, jaw, fists, and tummy. So many of us are tight beings doing work under tight deadlines.

But what if our bodies were more at ease? Easeful bodies doing work—that sounds so good to me!

In the time that gets assigned, please encourage your learner (and yourself!) to integrate that which supports unclenching. If we white-knuckle grip our way through life—what a recipe for exhaustion, lack of pleasure, strain, and even sickness.

I don't say that with judgement. I say it because I know and live this!

It is hard for our bodies to yield. To have a sense of safety, trust, and spaciousness, physiologically.

I don't say it comes naturally—it doesn't for me. So, I practice.

I practice through micro-moments of remembering to breathe deeply and invite my belly to soften; I practice through mindfulness over how much caffeine, sugar, and other on-the-go foods I'm eating; I practise through slightly longer scans of my body, head to toe, inviting each body part, through breath and awareness, to release whatever tension it can.

And I practise through an informal version of progressive muscle relaxation. To do this, when I'm feeling tense and in the grips of a time crunch, I inhale, clench my fists as tightly as I can for a few seconds, and then release the clench along with my breath. I follow this with a few easeful breaths, noticing through clench and release, I've relinquished some of the earlier tension. Then, with an inhale, I clench my fists and all my arm muscles, from forearm to bicep, hold, then release with the exhale, and savour the post-clench relaxation. After a few breaths and moments of awareness, I do the same with fist and arm, along with my shoulders, bringing them up to my ears, pausing, then exhaling and releasing. Again, a few breaths to follow. And, finally, from fist to arm to shoulder to now my face, fully squished and tense, like I'm dramatically reacting to the taste of something extremely sour, waiting, and then exhaling everything.

Try this out with your learner, and reflect before and after, whether there's any release of the earlier grip.

And consider conversations about what it's like, on the experience of—along with the final quality of—work done unclenched.

Raising time-aware learners

There's so much rushing. There's so much that's fast, frenzied, and sometimes even an out-control-feeling.

School doesn't *have* to be like this. At least not all of the time.

With your help, your learners can feel encouraged to relate to time a little differently. A little bit more awake, a little bit more spacious.

With that ease—of schedule, planning, and somatically—your learner can move through more work. They'll have greater capacity, and greater awareness.

It's not easy or immediate. But you'll be helping to recalibrate what's a lifelong dance with doing and productivity. One that you can help make healthier and more sustainable.

Chapter 2

Undoing Prioritisation Shaming

We've all said it. Or at least thought it. "If only you could just manage your time better!" Whether in thoughts or words, it comes out when we see our kids scramble to get an essay done—that they had two weeks to finish. Or when we're *all* late to get out the door to school—for the umpteenth time—our kids' homework and lunch not yet packed, one shoe bizarrely missing, and teeth unbrushed. Or, when an assigned book *still* hasn't been cracked open after a month, and now it needs to be read *and* reviewed by the next day.

And that thought, or phrase, "if only you could just manage your time better!" usually comes with the tone of a bark or yell. It's stern. It's exasperated.

I feel tense just thinking about all the times I've felt rushed alongside, or let's face it, totally because of my kids. Tense to recall the times when I have had to rush them, or "hurry up'd" them, or lashed out with a, "let's go already!" Always scrambling, maybe 'just' making it, and ever apologising.

Yet it's not totally one-sided. There have been times when I have made them late. Times when they have had to rush or wait for me. I admit these, and vulnerably too, to make open, honest space for us all to consider time. And how short and tight it is for every one of us. I have made those same mistakes as my kids. Haven't you?

I've forgotten to get my bag ready the night before. I've put off starting a task early, mistelling myself that there's "lots of time"—panicking at how "lots" has evaporated and now it's the night before a major presentation.

It still shows up in my life—I forget to charge my laptop before a talk, I neglect to jot down a to-do and have it out of mind until moments before it needs to be done, I resist starting a project because its deadline *looks* far off on the horizon, yet before I know it, find it near and looming.

Luckily, I *do* know better. I also know how uncomfortable that scramble feels. I have a body memory of trying to get a muti-week project completed in one night, of arriving in a grad school class having totally forgotten that a paper was due immediately, of trying to read a 450-page text in one night with a book quiz awaiting me the next morning. And these keep me committed to doing the work of prioritisation, to trying to learn as much as I can about why prioritisation continues to be so elusive and confronting, and to teaching what I learn, all in the hopes of more peace at home, more work done on time, and ultimately to know what to do first and next.

The other thing I'm committed to is avoiding that bark, that yell, that sternness. That. It doesn't mean I'm not frustrated when my kids aren't ready, or if they procrastinate. It doesn't mean that I don't have to take a breath—a deep one, or two—when my students request extensions because, they bravely admit, they didn't start a project in time. And, it doesn't mean that I don't get caught up in rush-rush-rush mentality once in a while, or, likelier, once a week—I do.

But in this chapter, I'll teach you different approaches and techniques that you can offer your kids, instead of barking your annoyance. Ways of thinking about priorities that can reduce chaos and frustration. And, above all, I'll bring clarity, logic, and strategies to what "prioritisation" really means, and how to do it.

Avoiding assumptions

Prioritisation is one of those words we're all *supposed* to understand. Definitions and plain language are always helpful, particularly when explaining something to our learners. This is *especially* true of words that are used frequently yet explained *infrequently*. "Prioritisation" definitely fits that bill. Kids are told to do it, adults are assumed to be expertly at it, and yet *what* is it?

Prioritising means to give order to the "stuff", the to-dos, one needs to get done. When we prioritise, we give *reason* and shape to what to-do we start with, what to-do comes next, and what to-do follows or can wait. We can do this for ourselves *and* teach this to our kids.

Why order? Why shape? If to-do lists are approached from top to bottom, there would be hard, weighty, complex tasks scattered throughout or clustered up. There's usually no rhyme or reason to how a to-do task list came to be—it emerges based on what occurs to our brain at that moment. So things done linearly are the opposite of prioritisation.

21

If to-do lists are approached based on first clearing what's easiest to cross off the list, sure, there'd be the pleasure of lots of checked-off and marked-as-done items, but they'd might be the lighter, swifter tasks, leaving the intricate, multi-step tasks until the end when energy and motivation are low. Straightforward to-dos—like writing a thank you email, folding laundry, or searching for a new phone plan—are more tempting to tackle than, say, a report with a looming deadline.

"Priority" is such an important word to move out of the shadows, and to provide learners with a handle on. There's an art to it yet is both so pervasive and ambiguous. Yet again, a key word, a key *concept*, is left generic and undefined for learners such that they don't know *how*.

Left as an expectation or judgment, shame easily enters in. It can feel embarrassing to ask *how*. It can also feel lonely and isolating. It can feel hard to pinpoint what's unclear when something is treated like a common, everyday word. Like, we should just *know*.

A starting point is to have a conversation with your kids about what "prioritisation" means to them. And to do some quick, fun, back-and-forth priority contrasts, like a family dinner with grandparents or a best friend visiting from out of town, both occurring at the same time, or preparing for a reflection paper and a group project due on the same day. (In a way, it's like a round of "would you rather" with competing invitations and demands in place of grossness.)

Interrogating importance

If prioritisation is about ordering to-dos, how is that done? What's the ranking based on?

Prioritisation is about ranking importance. Seems straight-forward enough.

On one hand, yes. On the other, it's wildly challenging—after all there is no singular "importance." It can be very difficult for a learner to know what's more important than another thing, and even what "counts" as important when so much of that impor-tance is determined for them.

There have been numerous systems created over the years—matrices, percentage-based tricks, and apps—that help students of all ages and years prioritise those "what's importants." There's the Urgent/Important Matrix, aka the Eisenhower Matrix or the Dump and Sift Method that plot the intersection of how soon something is due. There's the 80/20 rule, otherwise known as the Pareto Principle, that directs how much energy goes towards the most investment-worthy tasks. There are funny, memorable phrases, like "eat the frog," to clarify that the hardest task should be tackled earliest in the day. And there are all kinds of list-making phone apps with options for colour-coded flags to denote importance.

While each provides students with a helping hand to some degree, none provide a fulsome picture. None account for what's beyond the percentage point or due date as criteria in terms of importance. None take personal meaning into the equation or factor in the role of the teacher and what *they* happen to emphasise as crucial.

Importance is a tricky metric.

Sometimes, what's important has to do with your family's val-ues. For example, prioritising integrity and generosity as guid-ing principles. Or prioritising being on time, if not five minutes early for everything, as a gesture of honouring another's time and worthiness. There are too many "what's important" to name, and there are too many variables that go into informing one's "what's important" to list.

Compassion, being of service, giving back to one's community, saving 30% of what one earns, environmental activism, are just a fraction of some "what's importants." Some or all might be what's important to your kids, or to you. Or, you might have a completely different list.

Another element that popular prioritising systems leave out is capacity. What we have energy for in a given time frame.

So, now what?

The factors at play

Let's lay it all out for your learner.

What's important includes what's "worth" the most, grade-wise. So, something that is 30% of a course's final mark is more important than something that's worth 10%. In this way, importance is about *value*.

(As a side note, it's not that marks are actually important. It's that they're a contrivance we can't shoo away. They're real... in this artificial system. And we can't pretend otherwise. It's just that they're not the end all and be all, they're not entirely trustworthy, they're not indicative of a *student's* worth. So, ideally, we include this in the conversation too. They matter. But they're not everything. And a single grade is a snapshot in time, not an indictment or truth.)

What's important is also what's due soonest. In other words, importance also has something to do with urgency. If something is due tomorrow, it is "more important" than something that's due next week, at least in part. Now, we can't forget or push off for too long, what's due next week, but we do have some breathing room. In broad strokes, what's important is partly related to when something needs to be completed by.

This is where most strategies stop.

Let's keep going.

What's important is also connected to that which the student themselves feels is important. Where they're compelled. Where there's resonance. Where they're curious or even mesmerised. It doesn't mean that whatever it is that has them rapt has to go first, not at all. We need to find a way to honour it. Deep interest is one of life's best feelings, so we need to balance it with that urgency and value of something that needs doing.

What's important includes the body and capacity. We need to consider energy, injury, disability, the extra work and emotional labour for folks who face injustices, the exhaustion of caregiving or parenting, the fatigue of long commutes, and the zapped capacity from doing healing work, like psychotherapy, physio, or medical treatment.

So, when we talk about those "what's importants" to order and rank in service of prioritisation, we need to have this fuller picture.

Enter teacher

What's important also has to do with a teacher's aims. This is, in my mind, so seldomly spoken about. I have some reservations here, as I did with talking about the (complicated) importance of marks. Like high value assessments have to be prioritised given that grades are inarguably the currency of school, working to satisfy teachers' aims is also a crucial part of the picture.

For better or worse, a teacher wields a lot of power in a classroom setting—and while you or I might wish that to be different, it simply *is*. Sometimes, that can be wonderful. A learner might encounter a teacher who is an advocate or a mentor. Sometimes, however, it can be the opposite. Whether teacher-as-advocate, or adversary, in any schooling situation, there's some kind of instructor who is determining the texts, the rubric or grading system, the feedback, the tone—and that must be considered in our discussion of "what's important."

Am I suggesting that a student should contort their work just to satisfy the teacher? No.

Am I suggesting inauthenticity or placating? No.

I don't think it's a student's job to make the teacher feel better, to mollify them, or to put up with mistreatment. But I think it's important that a student understand that when "objectives" are articulated in a class, those are the objectives of that specific teacher in their specific jurisdiction. They are not fixed, true-for-all-time, true-everywhere aims. They are chosen, at least in part, by a person, department, or board. And that the person teaching has *their* priorities, their preferences, and certainly, their biases.

Often, those biases need looking into and pushing back against. But to do so, a student needs to see them and recognise what their teacher wants. And, from there, they have more of a choice of how to proceed.

My intention is not to get too philosophical here, it's simply to name that a learner can benefit from understanding their teachers' priorities, as they can help inform their own.

What's important? is a blend of what has the highest value marks-wise, what is due soonest, what's most compelling and resonant to the learner, what a learner has physical capacity for, and what holds meaning to the teacher.

From here, we are ready to take action and transform our to-do lists.

What to do when

Learners will no longer leave their overfilled to-do lists un-changed. We're moving *towards* something more refined and helpful, some way to go about it all that helps learners see what to do first, second, and next.

Let's imagine that on one particular evening, a student has:

- A novel study on the go—in specific reading historical fiction, a favoured genre—with one 15-page page chapter assigned to be read by the following day.
- A complex group project worth 35% that was assigned two months ago and has another month until a culminating presentation and slide deck are due.
- A midterm test coming up in three days that's worth 20% of the term's overall grade, and that their teacher continuously reminds is excellent practice for the final exam a month later.
- Two key chores for the evening, specifically walking the dog and putting away the clean laundry.

Let's also imagine that this learner is feeling overwhelmed. They've just come from their martial arts class, where they've torqued their back a little, and are worried that they'll have to work into the night. This means they'll go to bed super late and be exhausted the next day when their alarm goes off at 7am.

What do they do? What do they start with, how much time do they spend, and how will they get it all done?

Let's remember our five criteria:

- What's worth the most (%)?
- What's due soonest (mm/dd/yyyy)?

- What's most personally interesting (!)?
- What's their physical capacity to do?
- What's most important to their teacher (?)?

Now, the student's to-do list, without any prioritisation added, might look a little something like this if the items had been jotted as they were requested or remembered:

- Walk dog
- Read
- Study
- Laundry
- Group presentation

If the learner tackled the to-dos with this list left as is, the student might:

- Begin by walking the dog, which although a beautiful, important, and healthful activity on its own, risks pushing back the other pressing to-dos of the evening, risks adding further strain on their back, and misses an opportunity to take that same healthful walk yet as a break in the middle.
- Start on folding laundry as, next to the other items, is 'easier' and thus gets us to a crossed-off item, and all its emotional and cognitive satisfaction, sooner.
- Leave midterm-studying for another day.
- To that point, reading, working on a not-yet-due group project, and back to studying, they all have undefined qualities to them—without boundaries, they could take as long as the student sits at their desk.

- That group project could also wind up being last because group tasks, and the complexity of scheduling and collaborating, often feels like it takes longer and is thus less desirable.

So, how do we begin?

Let's bring a little bit more structure, clarity, and definition to these tasks:

1. Read 15 pages.
2. Group project—complete 2 slides.
3. Study by way of practising 5 questions, creating mnemonics for 4 definitions & explain 2 theories to a sibling/ parent/friend.
4. Walk dog around the block, now that back has eased.
5. Fold laundry until hamper is empty.

Here, we have not only what needs to be done, but also some shape to it so that we know what "doing" that task really entails. We'll get much deeper into this when we explore studying, but generic verbs and words don't help us start or move through tasks. If I write "read" down, but not how much *to* read, I will read until my eyes glaze over and I've stopped being engaged, or, likelier, about 15 minutes after that as it's very difficult to catch tuning out the moment it happens.

When we write down the number of pages, paragraphs, slides, or minutes, even if they're estimates, then we have a much less overwhelming starting place. We make things much more concrete.

We *could* even try to practise estimating how much time it might take to do those group project slides and all that goes into studying. And, give ourselves a bit of a limit to how long folding could take—especially if we ditched our phones and turned on some music as we did it.

Then, it would look like:

1. Read (15 pages).
2. Group Project (2 slides).
3. Study: Practice 5 questions (15 minutes), create mnemonics for 4 definitions (20 minutes) & explain 2 theories to brother/parent/friend (5 minutes each).
4. Walk dog (30 minutes).
5. Fold laundry (15-20 minutes).

Now, are we going to start with reading those 15 pages and end with folding? We can't say yet. These still aren't prioritised. Let's actually do the work of "prioritising" this list according to what we have named as actually comprising "most important."

1. Study: Practice 5 questions (15 minutes), create mnemonics for 4 definitions (20 minutes), & explain 2 theories to brother/parent/friend (5 minutes each).

I'm going to put this first for two reasons. It might seem, right off the bat, that I'm breaking my own criteria. After all, I noted that we have to prioritise what's of higher worth or value. This is true. Also, I included considering what a teacher emphasises as well in the mix of trying to prioritise. Above, I mentioned that the teacher had emphasised that the midterm, and thus the studying in preparation, was excellent practice for the final exam. By listening, your learner can glean the teacher's intent—the hidden suggestion to take this exam to heart to setup for the not-too-distant weightier exam.

2. Group Project (2 slides).

This is a big value item on the list. And because it's not due for another month, is easy to put off. Yet, because it was a three-month long assignment, and because two months have already passed, there are sizeable expectations about the final artefact, and a sense that, at this point, two-thirds of the work should be wrapped up. If we put off those two slides today, and tomorrow, we will run that too-common risk of trying to blast through a major, substantive project in too short a time, putting both grades and well-being at risk. By chunking this big project up into various, clear-cut sub-tasks, we can make steady progress and set ourselves up for likelier holistic success.

I'm suggesting doing this by slides because it can be hard to assign clear minutes per slide, after all, one might be more decorative while another more informative; and, depending upon your learner's skillset, one might take longer than the other.

3. Walk dog (30 minutes).

At this point in the evening, the most skillful next step might be to take a step back, or a step outside. To pause, move the body, switch from a mode of *doing* to a mode of *being*. Yes, the dog-walking chore is getting done, but as one close colleague always kindly reminds me, movement is additive, not subtractive—in that it doesn't *really* take away time, but rather when we move, we're adding energy, motivation, stamina, purpose, cognitive clarity, creativity, and a rejuvenated mindset. I would add, when we move outdoors. And, for all the dog-lovers reading this, heightened further when we tend to our furry family.

4. Read (15 pages).

What a delight! We return home from a brisk walk, or a slow stroll, feeling refreshed, and looking forward to our historical novel. You'll note that above, this was one of those tasks with resonance. One that's likely the easiest to "get done". Because of this, students might be tempted to do it first. But, then what happens? What's it like to look ahead to the rest of the night's work and see complex, multi-step, less desirable to-dos? Placing the task with resonance here has helped with the momentum of the evening.

If reading 15 pages, no matter how interesting the content might be, feels like a slog for your learner, then suggest chunking those 15 pages into three 5-page chunks. What would the learner do in between?....

5. Fold laundry (15-20 minutes)!

Tunes on, and if reading in chunks as above, one category of clothes at a time...as in, ball all the pairs of socks, then read another 5 pages, fold all of the shorts, read another 5 pages.... Yes, task-switching can deplete, but it can also *uplift* hard tasks too! Remember, there is no one way.

It's about what lands as helpful, motivating, and healthy for your learner.

At this stage in the evening, it feels celebratory. All the work has been accomplished, and it feels palpable because it all had a start and an end to it. It wasn't "reading" but, rather, reading 15 pages (potentially 5 pages at a time). It wasn't "working on my group project" to no clear end, but rather, 2 slides in the communal presentation slide deck. Even the dog, and your child, got some self-care-style TLC by taking a walk in the middle.

And they got to bed on time. High fives!

Careful calculation

You might be thinking that this is all a little bit elaborate for one night's worth of homework. And your learner might be thinking, "I have to calculate this *every day*?" Yes and no.

Here are my thoughts:

- Doing work this way—planfully prioritising according to those "what's important" factors—gets the work done in a humane, efficient way.
- When we get work done today, and then tomorrow, and then again the next day, we experience a sense of accomplishment.
- As we feel that accomplishment grow, our capacity and confidence grows.
- Then, we're on a roll—momentum is under way.
- I'll also add, this style of considering and ordering the several, and sometimes conflicting, "what's important"

demands is a form of project management, and that is a professional skill that only grows in complexity—you're giving your learner a highly useful and employable skill.

We also begin to internalise this way of doing work. Front-loading tough work, never putting off studying, being proactive and purposeful around healthful non-work breaks, and committing to a "little and often" or spread-over-time approach. After 50 times, 100 times, a year or two or five, the minute details become less important as it's now a habit, a rhythm.

Then again, when it works for your student, they may *want* to do this on the daily. I do!

Three things

Is that the extent of prioritising possibilities? Not at all. I'm aware that for some learners, the above will feel unwieldy, or overwhelming to try initially.

So, we'll try another approach that involves less ranking, less negotiating between whether one task is of more or less value than another, and more paring things down.

It also comes with a different skillset: boundaries. You might be reading more about the importance of learning to, practising, or insisting upon boundaries—for our own well-being—in our relationships, and in our work lives. Let's tap into the wisdom of boundaries for schoolwork.

What does this "Three Things" prioritisation approach entail?

It invites learners to focus on completing three things in a work evening or session. As in, which three things would be most skillful to lighten the mental burden, move them closer to completion, make a dent, support a shared project, or fulfil a commitment?

This approach comes with some potential fallout, but also profound skill-building, and potential for powerful ripple effects.

As for the fallout, by narrowing down this same evening, for example, it means that not everything will get done.

As for the skill-building, there are many. The skill of discernment—wise judgement—would certainly strengthen. Same with the skill of self-advocacy—knowing and articulating what one needs, including a balanced life. As well, the skill of agency—enacting what one wants and needs to have happen. The skill of planfulness would also become bolstered—as the three things that a student chooses for this evening will impact what three things would happen the next day. As in, a learner could elect not do the same three things today as tomorrow as the day following. They would have to decide on tonight's three things in context of when the other pressing to-dos get their turn.

As for the ripple effects, it could lead to greater balance for the student, deciding upon three things as the night's work, allowing them time for connection with family and friends, their body and healing, their hobbies and nourishing activities. It could also honour a student's pace, which might be to read things twice, to soundboard ideas verbally, to use adaptive technology and deal with any glitches that arise, to experiment with a variety of means and modes of expression, for example brainstorming with a different app, writing a report with a new approach, or trying a novel reading strategy.

"Three Things" might, for some students, allow for more spaciousness. It might also mean *more* time on each of the three items, which some students love. While many students might be keen to up their capacity for efficiency, others might be run-ragged by hyper-efficiency, and want or need to practise slowing down, taking instructions, and working at a slower pace.

I'm not suggesting "only" and "ever" three things—sometimes, that needs to budge, depending on the context. For example, during an exam study period, a post-secondary student has more space, so they might be able to take on three 'things' in the morning, and three in the afternoon. In summative periods, when independent studies and capstones and final presentations and performances and critiques and end-of-year projects wind up, three might be too limiting.

That said, if a student who has had an erratic, sporadic, inconsistent approach to getting stuff done, as in days (and days) would go by without touching any work, consistently getting three tasks done each evening would get this student much further—in terms of completing their to-dos, their sense of accomplishment, their marks, their confidence, and their motivation. They would certainly experience change.

And what a relief it can be for students to have as their guiding principle, "I just need to get three things done and then I can take the rest of the night off." Especially after a busy day of learning or navigating tricky friendships or balancing school with volunteer work or a part-time job or also training to be an athlete or engaging in mental health support. "Three Things" can be way of prioritising that keeps it simple.

Raising learners to prioritise

In a sense, prioritisation is the gift adults can give to their learners. How so? Because most of us weren't taught explicitly *how* to prioritise, but rather learned through experience—being late on things, losing marks, feeling anxious over deadlines, and barely reaching them.

Your learners will do *a lot* of experiential learning, but the basics of prioritisation—that rank-ordering—can be well-supported by you.

Will all your learning strategy hints and nudges land well? Of course not! You're their family!

But, remember, you're not saying what to do first. You're sharing how to *know* what to do first, how to *think about* and *plan* in intentional ways.

Their "what's importants" will be different than yours, and that's essential.

So the gift is that you're giving language to it all, normalising that it's difficult, making clear that it's a skill and not just an assumed capacity people have or don't have. You're making it okay to not know, and to be curious *to* know.

And ultimately, you're helping learners understand that they have choice, if only a little, and they can think about how to tackle their workloads in ways that are health- and well-being-oriented. That they can open up more space by thinking through what goes first, next, and last.

Chapter 3

To Plan or Not to Plan

This chapter takes an honest look at when planfulness works—
and when it doesn't. Moving through work in an ordered, intentional way can help tasks get done. But so can running with
times of immersive, deeply engaged flow. Too often, learners
wait for that engagement, that muse to ring the doorbell and
announce its presence, at the expense of just *getting to* a task
that needs doing—but arguably just as often, learners are encouraged *out* of creating the conditions for sticking with in-the-
zone times.

So far, you've heard about planfulness—and how to do it—
in a variety of ways. From strategies concerned with marrying
tasks to time, to approaches that help us filter and arrange
tasks so we know which to start and end with. But that's not
the end of it. You'll have a feel from the outset that *Raising
Well Learners* is not prescriptive—there is no singular way to
do things, define success, or be a student. As well, you'll have
felt by now that inclusion is central to me—I want to reach all
families, and all learners. And you'll also know that a holistic
approach, one that not just allows for but centres well-
being, sustainability, relationship, and wholeness, reigns
supreme here.

I bring this up because this chapter is devoted to *not* planning. To *not* insisting upon following-the-schedule day after day.

I'm not advocating for anarchy, for tossing out our agendas, or for never making plans. What I *am* inviting in, is that most delicious of all work states: flow. And, that can't always be planned for.

But, it's actually more than just flow, that in-the-zone state. I'm rooting for times when we're so immersed in what we're doing that we're lost in it, but I'm also rooting for times that are open, easy, spacious. *Un*planned.

Exit hypervigilance

One of the benefits of incorporating some spontaneity into our daily or weekly schedules is the alleviation of hypervigilance. If we plan things right down to the incremental, to the minutia, to the bathroom break, we're in trouble. If agendas are so tight that we're racing, scrambling, metaphorically or literally breathless, then something has to give. If a study schedule winds up stressfully accounting for minutes (over questions, courses, topics, or longer timeframe windows), then we might have missed the point.

All this kind of planning is, it's important to start out by saying, so normal in the rushing, busy-all-the-time culture we're in. I am speaking to this with humility, and with awareness—I am a person *often* rushing, *often* busy-all-the-time. It's an era of 40-, 50-, 60-, 70-hour work weeks, "side hustles," "grind culture," and extra gigs squeezed in. All of which are fair responses to prohibitively expensive housing, food insecurity, and inflation.

I'm not here to encourage anyone to work less or earn less. How can we ensure that we're well—that all that we plan for can be done in a way that we can sustain, and that sustains us.

Additionally, I want to keep an eye on what our kids are inheriting from our work styles. Do they see us give it our all in our work *and* take care of ourselves? Do they see us set boundaries around being reachable, see us be flexible and playful and break away from our schedules *some* of the time?

Hypervigilance is the experience of an always-scanning, always-worried, nervous, anxious state. It happens for a lot of reasons, including trauma. The pandemic certainly activated hypervigilance in many of us—leaving us extra cautious, checking for danger in our environments and lives.

This hypervigilant state is something that I see students of all ages and years wrestling with. Students who feel a constant state of flurry and frenzy, of never-enough-time, of go-go-go. Students who feel like there's no room for a break, a pause, a night off. I want to make sure that these learners are reached.

I also want to reach students who love to daydream, to mull, to putter, to create. Students who dawdle. Who doodle. They're not served well either by a too-tight plan.

So what can we do?

We can recognise, name, and keep an eye out for this hypervigilance. Watch for when it creeps up. Watch for when it takes over. You can notice if your child, for example, has dishes piling up beside them, feeling like emerging from their room to deal with their dirty plates and cutlery is going to take them away from their work. Notice when they haven't moved much. Notice if they're sleeping less. Notice if their body is showing signs of stress running rampant. And, talk about it. Not critically, not judgmentally, but perhaps inviting a student on a walk around the block, inviting a friend over, putting on an irresistible family movie—anything to interrupt a going-too-far planful energy.

But there are many other things we can do, ones that prevent this intensity, and ones that nourish that healthful, holistic track to learning that we're taking.

Going with what grips

As a first waypoint in, you might consider encouraging your student to go *with* their interests. Too often, we're constrained by time, assignments, and to-dos to the point that we can't *do* what we *want* to do. Sometimes, we rarely, *if ever*, get to do what we want to do.

I'm not suggesting that a student take their foot off the gas to the point that work is forgotten, commitments are dishonoured, or chores are ignored. What I *am* recommending is that students—all of us, really—give ourselves and each other permission to explore what we're curious about.

For instance, if your student is reading a book on Egypt for a novel study, and they become captivated to learn more about the pyramids, or the geography, a too-tight plan might keep them from investigating. If your student is looking for an online resource or book from your shelf or the public library and happens upon a totally unrelated text that captures their interest, can there be enough wiggle room on their agenda to allow for that?

Not every time. Not every night. Not in every circumstance. Midterms, finals, summatives, capstones, end-of-term critiques—these might not be contexts in which students will be able to find themselves with ample time to dive into unrelated or adjacent explorations.

Is it possible to allow some time for this purpose? It's important to incorporate flexibility into our plans, allowing freedom to follow what truly resonates. Even imagining this—for my kids, for the students I teach, for my parent clients, and for myself—my shoulders drop a little, my stomach unclenches. In going with what grips us, we can permit a little more of this breathing room, and resonance, a little more often, well-supported by a well-laid plan.

Going with what emerges

Another reason to un-plan? Spontaneity.

What if, while taking the recycling out, an idea for a new guitar melody, a revised song lyric, an interesting baking ingredient, or a DIY science experiment idea emerges?

What if, while folding laundry, a poetic line comes to mind, or a creative engineering solution pops up?

Great ideas, innovations, and novel connections can come at any time. And, can come more often if we allow them space to arise.

But where do these good ideas go if there's no space, no time, to engage them?

One idea is to have a creativity journal, physical or mobile, that serves as a house for those sparks, those what-ifs. Sometimes, noting them in this 'house' can be satisfactory enough—a metaphorical home or parking spot that can be turned to again when there's *more* time and *less* planned. Yet other times, when creativity is really flowing, we want enough time to actually dive in—to extend and elaborate that flash of inspiration. How sad it would be if we were so rigid in our planning that there was no wiggle room for prototyping the feasibility, edges, and alchemy of a juicy *what-if*.

43

That innovation, that creative *maybe*, is so much more than "just" an idea. It's your child's voice and style in action. It's their connection-making, sorting through, and synergising all that they've learned, whether consciously or not. It's their intuition getting a little airtime. It's the seedbed for future passions, endeavours, and careers. It's also fuel for their confidence—in the form of what makes them *them*.

To limit a spark because "there's no time" feels sad to me, and a little risky, if not dangerous. It's a misunderstanding of part of what goes into "what's important"—that aspect of what feels alive for the student. Much of a learner's day is about what others decide: when a child is young, their day and to-dos and chores are largely set for them; older students have strict timetables and course requirements; mature students have work-life responsibilities that often leave minimal time for creative exploration, for those alchemical possibilities.

So, in balance, in concert, in proportion to those well-considered plans, those skillfully outlined priorities, may there also be allowance, if not a fully unrolled red carpet, for the spontaneous, as-if-from-nowhere, magic-tinged creative sparks. They're not wasted time or plans gone awry.

Insisting on space

Having slight mobility in the schedule—maybe in the form of 15-minute buffers between each task, or a 45-minute window planned after school or following the day's work "just in case"—enables spontaneity and freedom of creativity. It also allows extra padding for greater ease and spaciousness.

How does this reconcile? Ease and space are made more possible through careful planning, and by not planning *too much*.

Not too many things in one day, not too much all at once, not too full a plate.

Without planning and prioritising, it's a free-for-all.

Tasks often get completed randomly, if they get done at all, leading to feelings of overwhelm. Through the prioritisation process we've been focusing on, we can prioritise unstructured periods. These open slots in our schedule can be used for rest, meditation, walking and talking with a friend, self-reflection, journaling, contemplative reading, or dedicating extra time to a beloved hobby.

Open time, to use as what feels right at that time, in that moment. *Un*planned time, on purpose, for who knows what.

What are the gains? An unwinding of the body. An easing of the mind. A relief from the feeling that all there is to life is work. An opened-up perspective in trying out new ideas. A replenished sense of well-being, having switched tasks, particularly if they're from cognitive academic work to non-school explorations. Refreshed balance, not to mention purpose.

Also in these in-between times, agency grows. Instead of using open spaces to go down YouTube rabbit holes day after day, they beg for and strengthen our decision-making. That "what do I want to do right now?" skill. That, "of all that I could do with this next half hour of open-ended time, what do I want to spend it doing?" discernment. They invite us to take some kind of action, or intentional *in*action. It's breathing space as much as it is inspired space.

How crucial, then, in all the careful architecture that we craft for our days, to include and protect spaces that are mindfully *not* architected, allowing for something else, something expansive, something nourishing to unfold.

45

Not too tight

Boundaried windows are inviting, restoring, and crucial for ease and spaciousness. These intentional off-times are not only for unclenching the body and mind but also serve as a humane means to mitigate or heal from various challenges.

Disasters happen. News of divorce. A flare in depression. An acute illness. Medication with overpowering side effects. An accident. They come usually without warning, and certainly *none* are according to plan.

Yet, if we're scheduled down to the wire each day, when do we prevent what we can, and when do we recover and heal from what we can't?

Learners who live with chronic illness or pain know that flare-ups are inevitable and will often know of variables like sleep, rest, connection, and nutrition that can *help* keep things in check—supports that offer no guarantee, just contributors to a greater likelihood of balance. But each of those things takes time: sleep needs a big, firm window that cannot be borrowed from to catch up on work; rest, different than sleep, needs to punctuate the day; connecting with family, friends, and community is so potent, and needs time for tending; shopping for nutrient-dense food and making healthful meals and snacks are time-consuming.

If we've too-tightly knit our evening of work, when will any of the above happen?

If we haven't enabled enough breathing room to sleep, rest, connect, and eat well, we borrow from our health, whether we live with a condition or not. We make a longer-term gamble.

It's not out of pessimism that I emphasise this. I'm not inviting disaster or disease. Rather, I'm trying to honour that living with a diagnosis can come with facets that require its own "homework" or workload. Even if undiagnosed, maybe there's burnout, grief, or loneliness that require care and time. Maybe there's bullying or a break-up.

I'm not equating or flattening these. Instead, I'm aiming to crack open the conversation about planning. About what we consider is "worthy" or "necessary" in an evening's schedule. Because of how supercharged and competitive academic entrances, scholarships, internships, and the job market appear, students often work themselves to the point of having little to no inner resources remaining. Add an illness on top, and now we're stretched thin.

What do we do about it?

In and around, amidst and between, all of the planned-for, prioritised to-dos, we dot in those activities that support wholeness and health. It might line up, like that dog-walking chore in the previous chapter, but it might not. Your learner might need to schedule in a biweekly therapy session, or a physio appointment, or a time to meditate, sketch, or share belly laughs over FaceTime with friends.

On the surface, these can seem irksome—and come with that curt voice, *you have to get your work done*! You might hear yourself questioning your kid's priorities. But may we all, child and parent together, learn to integrate those elements that keep us well, buoyant, and hopeful, in concert with our school or work to-dos.

Planning the unplannable

Why else should we plan for that-which-cannot-be-planned? I want to put a pitch in here for what I think of as the broad banner of "pop-ups." This could quite literally mean a pop-up event—your child's favourite vintage clothing store is hosting an event—but really, it's about any happening that's out of the blue. A childhood or family friend is coming into town for one day only or a last-minute appointment has come up after being waitlisted for months. Unforeseeable. Unplannable. And, unmissable.

So, how on Earth can we plan for what isn't plannable?

Sometimes, this can be booked in buffers, just like above. But, I think that considering both the disaster-planning just mentioned, as well as the pop-up foresight, that these are really like a trail of breadcrumbs leading us back to procrastination prevention and how we relate to time. If we can do work, prioritised strategically, when we *do* have time, energy, and capacity, then we allow room for the unexpected, whether challenging or fun.

I often advise students to refrain from working on Friday evenings and Sunday mornings as a hard and fast rule, encouraging them to keep these times open for rest and play. And, with these two blocked-off windows in the books, they can also be rejigged when needed. For example, if we've already planned our work to-dos around no-work Friday eves and the first half of Sundays, then we can swap those if something, say, pops up on a Thursday afternoon. Great! Take it! Make a swap! Take Thursday off but then work Friday evening.

It's possible that having only two dedicated windows isn't sufficient. In that case, make more! By increasing efficiency—such as reducing the time it takes to start tasks and opting for shorter, focused work sessions rather than lengthy, wandering ones—you may find room for more windows.

It's also possible that those two time windows are too much. I've worked with students juggling full-time Engineering, work, caregiving responsibilities, and applying to multiple graduate schools during final exam season. In such intense situations, prioritising well-being becomes essential, although incorporating fun may not be feasible. In these instances, we aim for smaller unplanned breaks and schedule larger ones once the peak workload has passed.

Flexibility is key! It's essential in our scheduling, in how we define and protect our free-time windows, and in our need to prioritise our well-being and spontaneous enjoyment just as we do our graduate applications and Biology lab reports.

Planning ahead for unplannable pop-ups can allow students to have a more balanced life, and an alive sense of joy, which are every bit as crucial as formal academic skills.

Fantastic flow

Flow is when we're immersed in and consumed by what we're doing. We lose track of time and sometimes other responsibilities such as eating. We're so in and *into* what we're doing that we want to keep going.

And why not? If you do a quick image search for "flow", it would take you a fraction of a second to locate depictions of flow that are described as "ecstasy." When we're in a flow state, that experience of being "in-the-zone", it is often equated as a type of ecstasy. Why? Because we're transported. Transported outside of ourselves.

Not outside of ourselves in a dissociative way but in a marvellous, losing-self-consciousness way. It's where we're not concerned about self-image, where our ego goes quiet, where we

49

don't edit or critique ourselves so harshly. It's generative, it's creative. We feel like we're on a roll. We just don't want to stop. Periods of being engrossed in something.

Too often, this is equated with the arts, but it can happen in any field, at any stage, at any age.

This is also not the same thing as addiction.

Nor is it the same thing as being entertained by something. Flow isn't about binge-watching or social media scrolling, unaware of time passing. One of the conditions for flow is deep, interactive engagement. It's not about leisure. It's work but work that is at the right challenge-level for our skills that once we start, we're fully immersed.

Why do I mention this? Because when we're in the grips of hypervigilant planning, where everything is too rigid, tight, restricted, accounted for, and metered out, we don't enable ourselves to experience flow or enable the conditions for it.

If we have to write a short story to present to a writer's group and get into a tear of writing, but have also left it such that there are five other things to do that evening because we're down to the wire, we can only craft 2 pages, no more. If we have those 15 pages of a novel to read, but our schedule's so strict and packed that we have another project to chip away at in exactly 45 minutes, we don't give ourselves the opportunity to fall in love with that book and keep going, even if that's what we long to do once we've started digging into that novel.

I'm not suggesting that there's full freedom to read for four hours the night before a major assessment. I *am* suggesting that pleasure of flow is worth considering allowing for by resisting too-rigid planning.

How, then, to invite flow, or at least the possibility of it? Back to that breathing room. And more to the point, back to our "time management" strategies that help us break down our tasks, prevent procrastination, and bring a reasonability and pace to our work. We're not left in a scramble. We're not left having to deny ourselves that pleasure, that ecstasy, of work that is so engaging, we get lost in it.

Raising for breathing room

I'm all for planning.

I'm also all for some *not* planning too.

Not planning helps us resist hypervigilance. It allows us the best way to follow what we're interested in, with full permission to be curious. It means we can be spontaneous and say "yes" to something we didn't see coming but are glad it showed up. It allows for flexibility, flow, and the delicious state of being lost in the best way.

Breathing room. Pacing. Buffers. Time for tending, and for prevention. Time to heal, and to recover. Time for fun, and for the unexpected. Time enough so that time can run away on us, if even a little, now and again.

PART TWO

GETTING INTO IT—HOW TO SWAP OUT MALAISE FOR MOTIVATION, DISTRACTION FOR CONCENTRATION, AND BOREDOM FOR CURIOSITY

In all that we want and hope for our kids, it can be dispiriting to see them with lackluster motivation, witness them fully unfocussed, and hear their complaints of boredom. Ooh, that's so tough—for them, and for you too!

But what gives me hope is that none of these are fixed. They're not immovable, they're not life sentences.

Unmotivation, distraction, and boredom can be shifted, if not completely turned around.

Now, it's not that our kiddos will experience deep engagement in every moment.

They won't have laser focus in every context or for every task.

They won't be riveted by every school to-do.

But your learner *can* move from languishing, malaise, and ennui, to finding their footing and participating more fully. They can grow in awareness of what steals from and what restores their capacity to concentrate. They can learn to sit with the discomfort of boredom without needing to have everything be entertaining *and* can find ways and workarounds to experience more interest.

Without learning strategies, our learners can feel stuck. They can feel like an aversion to boredom, or finding it difficult to pay attention, are truths about them. Like it's just the way things are. Like things that feel difficult will always be difficult in the same ways.

But your learners' ways of being, mindsets, capacities, and approaches aren't set in stone. Their experiences are for always. And there are so many things to try, to experiment with, to explore. Your learners just haven't been taught them before.

Will there be immediate change? Not necessarily. Although there could be.

Does your learner need to try everything all at once? Nope. It's a one or two at a time approach, little and often, over time.

Is it natural to feel resistance? You bet. Both from your learner, and your own. When things have been hard, for a while, it can feel difficult to believe that things can change. That school can go better and get better.

That focus can return, even if a bit.

That avoidance can be replaced by a return in motivation.

That "bored" might be a word you'll hear less of.

But it's more than possible.

Chapter 4

Caring When It's Hard To

It's easier to do schoolwork when a student is naturally interested in the material—when they're fond of the teacher, drawn to a reading, or whiz-like with problem-sets. But what happens when there's none of that effortless care? When, in fact, they *don't* care? When there's nothing easeful or engaging about the text or test?

Sometimes, we luck into the most interesting course with supportive, encouraging peers and deep class engagement—everyone is all in. And, there's *the* most compelling teacher—riveting, approachable, clear. The curriculum, the pedagogy, it's all been carefully, thoughtfully, intentionally considered—everyone has a way to access the class experience, the lessons are scaffolded and looped so that there's more than one chance to learn something, there are opportunities to experience and even inhabit the lessons; they feel personally relevant. The material moves along at what feels like a natural cadence—it's neither easy, nor out of reach with too much challenge, but rather is pitch perfect. And the assessments feel not just doable but purposeful—there's a sense that the assignments have a reason, are well-matched to what's been taught, the marking scheme feels fair, and the feedback is timely and supportive.

In this scenario—it wouldn't be hard to be motivated, to be engaged, and to care.

The challenge is, what if school *isn't* like this? How do we help our learners?

Is motivation only present for your learner when the conditions are ideal? What does it mean to be motivated an *un*motivated? How can we support our learners in caring about school when it's hard to?

I think "motivation" is both crucial and fraught to talk about, increasingly so. It feels hard to untangle from "incentivisation" —as in, "fill out this questionnaire and you'll have a chance at a $100 gift card!" Even if that questionnaire comes with the potential to have one's voice heard, to make change, to be helpful to ethical research—often, these don't feel very motivating, or not motivating enough. But, ooh that gift card! That's the ticket! (Sigh.)

With so much written about the science of motivation, the kindling of drive, the imperatives of grit, it feels tricky to discern what's truly helpful for our learners. What the overlaps and nuances are to motivation, and to the frequently related "engagement" or "drive."

Motivation has a kind of keep-going element to it, but that's not it entirely. Motivation has momentum to it, but again, not only. Motivation has want and desire, but usually in context when those wants and desires are to *not* do the task at hand, but to do something else.

In this chapter, I'm considering motivation as the spark or the starting point of *why* we do something, *before* we actually start it. It's the reason, the push, the *motive*.

It sounds simple, but it's not. In many parts of the world, including where I live, attending K-12 school isn't really a choice. It's mandated by law or societal norms, so students have to go regardless of their personal motivation. They don't need to think about *why* they're going to school or why they would *want* to; it's expected of them. (It's crucial to name how many learners around the world can't go to school, whether because of political regimes, gender barriers, family financial pressures, or *in*access of any kind. Equally notable is just how much learners *want* to go to school...when they can't.) I carry these learners, near and far, in my heart, and yet am aiming to reach parents of learners in the reverse situation: who *can* attend school, who *are* in classes, who *do* have projects and tasks they are accountable for, and yet don't feel motivated.

In North America, attending K-12 school is usually mandatory. However, when it comes to higher education like college, internships, or other types of formalised learning experiences, you often have more freedom to choose whether to participate, although people expect or assume that you will. Sometimes, families insist that you pursue these opportunities.

We could keep going with local norms, and both close and global exceptions, but my point is this: there are lots of schooling spaces where motivation doesn't actually "matter" in that a student still has to go. That's where I want to make change; when a student has to do something, or go somewhere, but doesn't want to.

Now, we all know that a student can "go" somewhere without really "being" there. I can attend a lecture or event, but because

I don't have a want or a why or a motive, I might not be present and open to all that's being offered.

It's like hearing without really listening.

So, we're not really talking *willingness* to go or do, but *wanting*. Not *carrying on*, as so many posters love to keep riffing— *Drink Coffee, Carry On*—but *caring*. Caring, when it's hard to.

We'll focus on how to locate that care and how to tap into it, grow it, and borrow from it when it feels absent and when a class or school experience feels pointless and *un*motivating.

Find the start

When did your learner's demotivatedness start?

Whether by conversation together or by private journal, ask your learner, when they're in a moment of deep disengagement, or when they're open to diving in with you about their experience, that they feel might be the start of this *disinclination*.

Was there a discouraging moment with a teacher? Was there a time when something felt *particularly* difficult, like a hitting-the-wall lesson or class, that has felt like a discouraging force ever since?

Let me explain why I recommend starting this way. During a one-on-one session with a 12th-grade student-client, she shared that she was feeling very unmotivated and uninterested in her schoolwork and was not completing much of it. Her mom had seen me give a workshop on learning strategies to high school students and reached out because her daughter was part of the same community. Interestingly, the daughter hadn't felt like participating in the workshop that day, but her mom found it helpful and wanted me to help her daughter.

In doing so, quite early on in the rapport-building, I asked about this "lack" of motivation as she put it.

She paused when I posed the question, thought for not more than a moment or two, and then pinpointed not just to when, but *why*. She'd had a serious sickness right at the start of the school year. It took her out of classes for the first three weeks.

When she went back, still regaining her strength, she felt lost.

I felt her words hit me right away. Imagine that, feeling lost right from the start.

Of *course* she felt unmotivated. Who *wouldn't*?

From there, being quite literally disengaged, the bridge back felt to her as too big to cross. It's not that she didn't have enough "fight" in her, or enough grit. It's that the distance was too wide. The ripple effects were predictable in some ways: she skipped a few classes, avoided several assignments, made it look like she understood, and found presentable excuses for her teachers. Why? Because she didn't know how to do the work (and did not know how, or didn't feel safe, to express this). It might not always be so linear or singular. Perhaps there were a cluster of moments that might also come from a number of different contexts.

Demotivation might also be born from outside the school context—and school is where it's showing up. I have met students whose parents are going through a divorce, whose siblings are going through illness, whose beloved family member passed away—and these painful experiences can naturally evoke existential questions about the "point" of any of it. What *would* be the point for a given assignment or test for a student going through profound injury or loss?

61

It's not that there is none. It can just be hard to feel. Learning strategies help to repair that gulf and support learners in finding new sources of motivation—"hows" that support new "whys."

Find the what

Caring about something doesn't have to come naturally. It's okay that it's hard for some learners; and it's also important to note that it can be practised, learned, and felt little by little over time. It doesn't have to just *exist*.

This is probably a *very* inflammatory example but...ooh, I'm a little bit scared to share...here's goes...I didn't love my dog right away. (I'm so sorry for all the doggo folks reading this! I love her now, promise! Keep reading, things take a turn for the much better!)

It was a year into the pandemic and our two young ones had been aching to get a dog, so much so they played being puppies for each other—paws up and panting. It wasn't a whim, it wasn't arbitrary, but the actual getting-a-dog moment happened quickly.

When we first brought Zoë home, she was just a tiny puppy, and oh, was she adorable! She would sleep peacefully cradled in my girls' arms, melting our hearts with her cuteness.

And then she peed all over the house.

And then she bit everything, everywhere.

And then she scratched our arms up to no end.

I'd been raised with a cat and she didn't do stuff like that, so this was new to me.

And as I was on a Zoom work call, interrupted every two minutes by my then 5- and 7-year-old asking for help with their respective online classes, my lovely husband, also online, filled the room with his booming math teaching voice because Zoë piddled on the floor. I became *acutely aware* that I'd just signed up to take care of another being.

I've done *a lot* of taking care in my life. And I hadn't put the puzzle pieces together beforehand of *that* part of getting a dog. I was all in for the walks. But the yelping and indoor accidents while already doing the fractured-concentration online work thing, was overwhelming.

But, I can truly say, I came around. I *learned* to care for Zozo.

Please don't misunderstand, I wasn't unkind or dismissive of her, I didn't mistreat her in any way. But I didn't immediately care deeply for her, and in fact felt taken aback—normal, as I now hear, for a first-time dog owner—with the work and *un*pleasantness involved underneath all that cuteness, especially in the early days.

What were my *ways into* caring for her? I watched my kids fall in love with her. I thought about what a good decision this was for them and all of the joy (mid-pandemic) and the responsibility (life skills) that this was bringing. I actively savoured sweet times when things were easeful with Zoë for a moment, or in wonderful memory-making times together.

In other words, I *practised* caring. And kept on doing so until it took. And now? I utterly and unabashedly adore her.

This isn't so different from a learner in a school context. There might be one class (or more) that your learner feels, or states outright, "I just don't care about it." Maybe it's an off-putting teacher. Maybe it's lacklustre texts or lessons. Maybe it's a course that they have to take but don't have a natural love for. Maybe they feel alone, made worse by their dearest friends being placed in a different course but all together. It's unpleasant for one or many reasons.

So, then, we need to *find* things *to* care about.

And having a good "what" can help.

We welcomed Zoë into our family most of all for our kids whose worlds had been turned upside down, like everybody else's, with the pandemic. What were we doing? Giving our kids a heartfelt wish, not knowing how things would turn out in the larger world. We were giving them a healthful IRL distraction given the hours of online school. We were ensuring that we would be out three or more times a day—when playgrounds were caution-taped off. Those were the "whats" that we cared deeply about—fulfilling a long-held wish, and a health-promoting way to learn experientially.

In the case of your learner not caring about a class they have to take, what's in that class that they can find to practise caring about?

Is it a particular text, even one, that might be fulfilling? Is it in practising a new way to carry themselves or participate? Maybe it's a skill? Maybe it's about content? But what's the one thing your learner could find as their way in?

For example, if scholarly writing has been a challenge, maybe that's the "what." If professional communication has been a bit messy in the past, like in writing emails to teachers or profs, maybe that's the "what." If it's about struggling with recall on tests, maybe it's trying out different memory techniques.

A good "what" to care about can be directly or indirectly related to the class that's feeling *hard* to care about, and can go a long way to either getting your learner through, or maybe giving them a way to grow their care over time.

Find the who

When a class is leaving a learner cold, another way to find their care and motivation can be to suggest that they find their *people*.

Nudge your learner to—if the class is obligatory, and attendance and participation are essential—to seek connections in class.

Most often, the response will be something like, "no way," "I can't," "I don't know how," or "it doesn't work like that." As if parents aren't aware of what it's like to be in a dull class, feel awkward starting a conversation with someone new, or navigate social situations with unspoken rules about popularity and cliques.

But we do know. And also know that finding kinship, a soft landing, and a warm smile can make a big difference not just to how a class feels, but to making it there in the first place.

We've talked lots about this in the context of belonging, but there are ways to start that connection that are pretty low stakes, like talking about:

- A principal's announcement that just popped on the PA system.
- What they'll be doing for Intersession, Reading Week, or March Break.
- The weather if it's a particularly inclement day.
- Seeing them on the same public transit and asking whereabouts they live, and then talking about a favourite coffee shop or store in the neighbourhood.
- Something that you've been asked to read or do for class.

The beginnings of a bond can also start with:

- Grabbing an extra item being handed out for the person beside you as a small gesture of thoughtfulness.
- A genuine compliment if there's something they're wearing or doing that you find lovely.

None of this is weird. It's the way strangers can become less so to each other.

What might surprise your learner is that others in the class might also be struggling with disengagement. Or, more surprising still, is that someone else in the class that your learner might find an absolute struggle to make meaningful sense of is a peer's favourite class.

That can be magic.

How is it that the same class can land so differently? Well, when your learner makes a pal or two in that class, they can ask! "What is it you find so interesting?" "How do you like this class, I genuinely want to know...because I'd like to also, but am having a tough time?" (Or even, "how can you stand it?!?!") Your learner might hear aspects of the class—the teaching style, the material, the texts—in a whole new light. One that shifts the perspective of your learner.

Finding a person and hearing their different take might be the key to unlocking your learner's engagement.

Find the heart

Even bigger than finding *specific* tasks to make a class worthwhile or people to connect with is to find the deeper—deepest—value in the course, particularly if it's a struggle to engage.

Value-finding being key to a learner finding their care, desire to participate, and willingness to keep showing up.

In other words, what's in it for them?

Not as in a grade. Not as in an external reward as motivation. But the worthwhileness of it.

Here's what I mean: I will forever remember how a student of mine, years ago, turned his least favourite / most demotivating class, into a deeply meaningful experience. To do this, he made it so that every boring lecture, every disengaging reading he was required to do, every test and exam served as practice for when he was going to be a professional in his community.

He envisioned it in full detail, picturing how he'd use the topics (no matter how lackluster), the quiz material (even though he really couldn't give a toss), to help and support his community. It was nothing short of remarkable.

And, the *further back* backstory is that he'd failed the course. Twice. But it was a mandatory one. He *had* to make it through.

So, through these creative learning strategies, he found a way to find the value—for him, lifting his family, friends, and neighbourhood.

He saw himself as a practitioner, and each item he learned, he brought care to it by way of living as if he were already in that professional role.

How could your learner do that?

Sometimes I like to talk with learners, deep in uncaring, about this course, teacher, and series of readings and assessments as stepping stones. They're moments, encounters, and practices en route to their larger aim.

And it's not that a learner must pinpoint "what they want to be when they grow up." It can simply be their inclination. Like a knowing that they want to create art or music, or a leaning into building, or a hint that they're drawn to working with children, or a desire to be close to animals as a job. It doesn't have to be a defined career path—like a veterinary technician. It can be a sense, and from there, you can ask your learner, "how might this course, as uninteresting as it feels, serve as a stepping stone on your way?"

Is it how to keep showing up in tough situations?

Is it that the content is a precursor to the class they're *really* excited to take?

Is it that this course has introduced them to a subject area that they can confirm they really don't want to pursue, thus freeing up other avenues to explore and experiment with?

It can be as small and grounded or as spacious and indirect— what's the larger meaning for your learner?

Occasionally, a learner simply doesn't care—not only about a particular class but also about school, friends, and perhaps even life.

What a tough spot. So painful. For the learner struggling, and for their loved ones, worried and perhaps missing when their learner *did* care.

If your learner is having a hard time caring about anything, or if they're not finding pleasure in things, then learning strategies may not be the right, impactful, or most appropriate course of action.

Like any suggestion in this book, or any of my writing, required is a kind of openness, even if slight, and even if it evokes an initial sarcastic resistance.

When there's absolutely no openness and a persistent lack of caring, it's time to reach out to a trusted healthcare provider with expertise in mental health.

In my time as the lone learning strategist on campus for students with disabilities—mental health, learning disability, sensory, chronic illness, acquired brain injury, ADHD—I met and worked with hundreds of students who were experiencing depression, anxiety, and more.

When they experienced flares in symptoms, they had "their person," their therapeutic ally. And when their protocols or prescriptions were set, then there was capacity and interest to tackle school.

One lovely boss along my journey would always—I mean *always*—remind me and all those he supervised, "health first." I really appreciated not just the sentiment, but the repetition of it. The vocalness of it.

So, to you I share the same. If uncaring is deep, "health first," including mental health. If there is prolonged joylessness, if there is refusal to go to school, if there is no pleasure in anything, seek support. School will come. But there might be a resourcing or recalibration required for your learner first.

We can help by redirecting our efforts sometimes from the pressure of "you don't want to fail" or "don't lose the credit" or "you'll be behind your friends" to "let's take care of your well-being first" and "there's always time." There really always is.

In my earliest years as a high school teacher, I worked at a radical alternative school that welcomed learners of all ages who'd had their journey disrupted for all kinds of reasons, and there was such a readiness and joy to be there. The learners were open.

Now, there are online options as far as the eye can see, sometimes even free virtual credits, across the levels and years, and at many different starting dates.

There are options.

Remember, health first. And it's not that health needs to be perfect—impossible, no such thing. Nothing needs to be "solved" before starting with learning strategies or to re-engage in school. They can co-exist; they can mutually support each other. But I encourage your intuition and keen eye and close watch of your learner—if something feels off, if there's a heaviness of spirit that isn't lifting, if "I don't care" is palpable day in and day out, extra support to help them care again might be priority number one.

Raising carers

Sometimes, a learner lucks into a class that just feels resonant. There's a vibe, students' interest is held, it's easy to be all in.

My interest, in this chapter, and as a learning strategist is to give you as many possibilities for the *how* when things *aren't* easily engaging.

And, ultimately, to ensure that there are *things to try* when it doesn't so easily go in a learner's favour. It can't come down to whether a teacher is interesting or not; or funny, or on top of the latest edu-tech trends, or, or, or.

Ultimately, the aim is to provide *things to try* when things don't go smoothly for learners. It shouldn't depend on whether a teacher is interesting, funny, up-to-date on the latest educational technology trends, or any other specific factor.

I understand the various reasons why a teacher, just like a learner or parent, might be having a difficult time, such as health issues, personal losses, new responsibilities, or experiencing harassment.

None of these are the responsibilities of the learner. It's not for a student to hold. But if there's a more fulsome *approach* of care—an *ethic* of care—that becomes the starting place, we can take more responsibility for our own engagement.

There's so much teachers can do to *keep* their students. To inspire, to uplift, to grab their minds and hearts. Just as there's so much they can do to the opposite impact, sadly.

What has me forever-riveted is how to help make things "better"—lighter, less stressful, more interesting, more doable for learners to support their own leaning in—when it's not so easy to feel motivated.

When a learner is checked out and says with words or body language that they don't care much about their class (or course) (or program) (or teacher), I want parents and families and community carers to have things to say and, if there's openness, to suggest.

Chapter 5

How Stella Got Her Focus Back

If we get to the heart of learning, not much can happen if learners aren't paying attention. If a teacher is talking, but a student is spaced out, little to nothing is being understood. If a student is trying to make their way through a dense and intricate reading, or they're "listening" to an assigned podcast, yet their minds are distracted, nothing is being absorbed.

Focus is at the centre of just about everything to do with school, whether it's studying, or deep into creative, generative work.

Putting our attention on listening, remembering, recalling, on making something new, writing, or editing—all requires some degree of sticking to the thing at hand. The sometimes impossible-feeling challenge of directing attention on something and *keeping* it there.

In this way, this chapter might be the most important one for you to explore. It's about how to help your learner get back to the present moment, and get back to whatever learning is *supposed* to be happening.

Part of why it's so important to have as much focus on our side as possible is to process whatever teachings are being shared —whether it's through someone speaking, a group presenting, a text we're supposed to be reading, someone else receiving critical feedback that could help our own understanding, or any number of permutations of learning situations.

We need to have our attention with us in the moments an assessment is unfolding, so that we can bring all that we have heard, read, practised, and remembered. Like when we're facilitating a seminar, writing a quiz, or performing something. We need to be really there, in the moment, gathering and articulating and applying all that we can.

Being fully present is also incredibly helpful because it's efficient. For example, if learners are "in" an online lecture but not really paying attention, they'll likely have to go back and watch it again. This means spending more time on the lecture than necessary, maybe even *twice* as long. However, if learners are focused, they reclaim time for other activities like health, play, finding joy, and connecting with others (the very things that help to *support* strong concentration).

How can we do this reclamation of free time if we're having to double up the workload? They're incompatible! To wander in focus is to lose out on time for other more enjoyable activities!

There are experiences, sometimes diagnosed, increasingly common and particularly challenging for many students:

- Attention Deficit Hyperactivity Disorder (ADHD), a neurodevelopmental disorder characterised by persistent patterns of inattention, impulsivity, and potentially hyper-activity, which taken together notably impact function-ing and development, particularly in the forms of time management, impulse regulation, task organisation, and focus. There are three buckets of ADHD presentation, predominantly inattentive, hyperactive-impulsive, and combined. Hyperactive-impulsive presentation comes with things like being fidgety, restless, having a hard time sitting still, interrupting, struggling with awareness of consequences, and patience.

- Attention Deficit Disorder (ADD), the historical name for ADHD without the element of hyperactivity. In the most current DSM (Diagnostic and Statistical Manual of Mental Disorders), ADD is not used anymore. Rather, ADD is taken to mean the "inattentive" type of ADHD, or the non- or less-hyperactive-impulsive presentation of ADHD. For-getfulness, distractedness, organisation, follow-through, and focus are key challenges. Combined brings together both the hyperactive-impulsive and inattentive symptoms.
- Variable Attention Stimulus Trait (VAST), is a non-diagnosis but very helpful term that aims to push back against the medicalisation of attention challenges and honour how widespread they are. VAST honours that it's not that folks can *never* focus, but rather that it changes; to that end, VAST works in pairs. There are times when someone is unfocused, and in other times, hyper-focused. There are times when someone is bored and checked out, and other times deeply curious.

From a neuroinclusive perspective, there is a remarkable range of experiences, cognitive superpowers and stumbles, and human behaviours. There are so many individual differences in terms of how brains function, and also, in a collective sense, so much to marvel at.

Whether your learner has a formal diagnosis or not, whether you suspect that there's something intrusive going on, in no way am I suggesting that paying attention is easy. Nor am I suggesting that we can live in a constant state of focus. And I'm definitely not suggesting that concentration has the same reachability for each person.

It is difficult, it is messy, it is all over the map for folks, and it is dependent on so many factors.

Yet, even with so many individual differences and how challenging attention can be, I don't *not* want to talk about it. I don't want to *not* offer *some* strategies that *could* potentially lighten the load and bring glimpses and glimmers of attentiveness back to your learner at least a little more often.

There isn't one parent or teacher I've coached who doesn't lament student distractedness—or their own. Rampant and ruthless, distractions take us off-task and off-course, sometimes for hours at a time. But, despite how potent and prevalent they can be—there's so much that can be done to bolster concentration.

When you do

If your learner finds it challenging to stay focused, taking time to reflect on *when* they attempt to work on their tasks can be highly beneficial.

You can do this by swapping judgment for strategies to experiment with that are benign, creative, and helpful.

No one strategy will "solve" everything. And, our learners *aren't* problems to solve. Not every strategy needs to be tried.

And, trying everything just ratchets up the very overwhelm that learning strategies soothe and quell.

So, a first focus-healing strategy is to deep dive into the "when" of their work.

Focusing is hard. And to have it come online, alongside motivation, energy, stamina, creativity, curiosity—this can ask a lot of a learner. So, put the hardest work earliest in the day.

Does that mean what's hardest should come first? Not necessarily. I'm a BIG fan of medium-hard-easy. This is where your learner starts with something that's medium hard for both brain-readiness and to get a sense of accomplishment early on. Most students order their work, whether intentionally or not, easiest-medium-hardest. But who wants—or can—do the most complex work at the end of the day? Hardest, then, could come second. But ideally, it's not last.

Start with harder, end with easier. This can contribute a little to our capacity to pay attention.

How you do

You've got the when, now for the *how*.

Time blocking can be a helpful way to schedule and secure time to *do* focused work. Instead of your learner keeping a running to-do list beside them as they work, tackling it "as and when" encouraging them to block time off in their calendar *for* specific tasks is the key.

I call this "Task-to-Time Alignment", and go into detail in my book, *Feel Good Learning*. On the one hand, time blocking is a well-loved strategy as it boundaries windows in a calendar for work. On the other, it's really assigning or *aligning* tasks to those time blocks that makes them so useful.

It means moving away from scattered and eternal-feeling to-do lists and moving *toward* clear, set-aside time for specific tasks.

In this way, a little bit of focus is preserved in that a particular time is blocked for a particular task. No more wondering, "what should I be doing right now?"

Another key strategy with time blocking, or task-to-time-alignment, is ensuring buffer zones after or between blocks. This way, if something is taking a little longer, it can. Or, if your learner accomplished their task, they don't have to jump into the next one immediately. They can engage in some focus, and whole well-being, restoration.

How much you do

It can be very hard *not* to do the whole of something. But, for both focus preservation and for well-being, encouraging learners to leave something hanging for the next work session or day can be a helpful strategy.

Why?

Leaving a little behind is great for memory when it comes to studying. It's what's referred to as the Zeigarnik Effect. It's when we leave something interrupted or incomplete, and the beauty is that the mind keeps going. Processing is happening behind the scenes.

Leaving a little behind is great for helping to get back in the following day. We have a clear start by continuing or finishing what was started.

Leaving a little behind is great for energy preservation as well. Sometimes, we can do too much on one day and that robs our capacity and focus the next. This is always in tension, and it's a fine balance. There's no "getting it right," but there is an attempt. What is "enough" for today such that tomorrow is set up well for another day of enoughness.

And part of leaving a little behind is understanding the power of aggregates. Sometimes, learners—and all of us—race to get something all done, to "get it over with," to "be finished with it," to "move onto the next thing." But learners—and all of us —are better served by doing that thing over a longer time span. That notion of "little and often" is important.

Like an essay written 150 words at a time over 10 days, or a test studied for 10 practice questions a day for 20 days, or like a big presentation worked on for 15 minutes a day, 5 days a week, for a month.

The first day of writing those 150 words, it won't feel like much is getting written. And confidence for a test won't come with 10 practice questions, or even 20. And the first week of 15 minutes towards that presentation won't result in a sense of readiness. But the aggregate, the build-up, the total over time, *that* will feel great. Those shorter bursts may keep and maintain more attention than a 5-hour writing session to try and blast through an essay in one night.

"Little and often" adds up quickly, preserves energy, fuels next-day work, and facilitates focus.

How many things at once

Multi-tasking.

There's a lot of energy around this word.

On one hand, there are countless articles and hacks offered to improve and amplify one's ability to multi-task—to get more done in less time. On the other, there are folks denouncing multi-tasking saying it's absolutely impossible.

Then there are those who opt for the language of mono-, solo-, uni-, or single-tasking. But, back to the how and why I'm here with offer after offer of learning strategies—this is hard for so many folks. A shift in language doesn't come with a revelation of how to do this.

What I find most helpful is to talk about keeping focus unfragmented. To concentrate on one thing at a time without getting distracted. So, how can we do this?

The first piece that parents can help learners with is to share of their own experience of what fragments their ability to pay attention:

- Is it tabs on their computer that seem to multiply?
- Is it sounds that distract?
- Is it *too* much silence?
- Is it the physical discomfort of a space?
- Is it a disorganised space?
- Is it mental chatter?
- Is it in the body, like a bouncing knee or incessant knuckle-cracking, or someone else's?
- Is it energetic, like a flagging, tired energy that leads to dispersed or diffused focus?

This isn't an exhaustive list but is a good place to start. For each one identified, there are things to do and try.

- If it's about tabs: a learner could try either an artificial cap, like no more than 3 tabs, or practice "tab-grouping," which most web browsers have, enabling related tabs to be batched together and shrunk to the size of one, and able to be re-expanded at any time.

- If it's about sounds: earplugs or white noise can be a superb work-support, in fact most of the book was written while I was wearing earplugs.
- If it's silence: ambient, lyric-less music that's on a playlist, instead of DJing one specific song after another, can help hone focus.
- If it's space: at the end of a workday on a weekend, taking time to rethink and rearrange whatever furniture is at play can be a helpful endeavour to make focused work more likely.
- If it's organisation: likewise, taking time to declutter, refile, cull, upcycle, donate, repurpose, are all useful, ensuring that this comes at the end of a week instead of the night before a test.
- If it's physical: taking that restless feedback and devoting or channeling it to movement, before or mid-way through a schoolwork task.
- If it's energetic: a careful sleep audit can reveal whether enough—or enough sound and deep—sleep is being had each night and whether that could be a key factor.

What you do in between

What a learner does before school or a lecture, between classes, following a day on campus, between work tasks can help hone concentration, or (further) fracture it.

It may be the most critical factor in terms of what replenishes, or diminishes, your learner's attention.

Learners might have as their barometer for the day things like "just gotta make it through these three classes" or "gotta get started on that project" or "there's no way I can pay close attention in reading that long article." With an attention-prioritising approach, we can encourage our learners to ask instead, "what can I do right before each of these three classes to help me pay better attention?" Or, "what can I do before starting and halfway through working on that project to keep my concentration at its best?" Or, "what can I plan to do right after that article read that will sustain my focus?"

And what kinds of things can your learner do in asking about the befores, in-betweens, and afters that directly enhance concentration?

- Strategic movement.

Whatever way a learner likes to "exercise" or take up space with their bodies is best. Now, there's no one way a learner needs to move. It's not about particular movements. But rather moderate movement done at purposeful times to uplift alertness—moderate both in intensity and in duration. The key is to support your learner in contemplating *when* movement might be best. Is it at the start of the day to hone attention, or is it before a particularly challenging class in terms of boringness, that makes it hard to keep focused?

- Balance challenges.

In a pinch, if a neighbourhood jog, campus gym session, pick-up game on a community court or rink, or self-guided yoga session at home aren't possible time-wise, a mid-activity break to challenge balance can do wonders. How to do this? One way, if available to your learner's body, is to have them stand on one leg and slowly take off a sock and put it back on, all while wobbling and trying to maintain equilibrium. Then switch legs. Or, to stand on one leg and place objects on the floor and then pick them up, one at a time, bending down to place something down, like a card or marker, and then standing back up. You can do this with your learner, side by side or mirroring each other, and ask for a focus-check before and then after, having them reflect on any changes to their concentration levels.

- Nature Time.

Whatever your environment, whether lush or urbanly barren, get your learners moving outdoors. It's not that there's emerging research but copious, well-established, and robust bodies of research about how much time in nature can hone our focus. It doesn't have to be vigorous movement, it doesn't have to be beautiful, it doesn't have to be wild; it can be landscaped, it can be in the centre of a city, it can be a slow amble. Wherever there's nature, even if slight, nudge your learner out in it. Look at the sky, hear a bird chirping, feel snow, rain, or sunshine on skin. There are few things as potent as time outdoors, not doing anything in particular, just letting our very human inclination to notice fascinating things in nature, all of which come together to result in a remarkable restoration of concentration.

More than pushing through building distractedness, restlessness, or fogginess, restoring attention is key, and it's possible. Maybe not fully for all learners, and again, not all the time, but we're looking for incremental change which over time can build. Windows of time where cognition feels like it's on, crystal clear, and directed.

What you do when you're not working

In other words, sleep.

When learners don't get enough, or enough *good quality* sleep, they can't concentrate as well.

This is often my starting place. Students might be coming to my coaching sessions with questions about time management, studying, or motivation; I will almost always start with sleep.

How is your learner's sleep? Now, I won't go into the full sleep picture here as I've got an entire chapter on that, but I would be remiss not to bring it up here.

Cognitive function, including remembering, making sound decisions, and attentiveness is impaired when we don't get enough sleep.

When we don't get enough sleep, our efforts can be in vain. All the studying and active recall might not fully pay off because we miss out on the important processing that happens while we sleep. It's like we're depriving ourselves of extra study time that occurs during sleep.

When we don't get enough sleep, it's harder to be alert and all in when in class or working on a project.

When we don't get enough sleep, brain fog can set in, and instead of clarity of thought are things like mental, and physical, sluggishness. Our productivity and performance diminish.

When we don't get enough sleep, our range of executive functioning is impacted. From planning and prioritising to organisation and impulse control, all of it has an imprint from lack of sleep.

When we don't get enough sleep, the overwhelm that might be humming at a low level is amplified, the volume of our worry gets turned up, and the full spectrum of emotions are louder.

If we're not sleeping well or sufficiently, then focus suffers. So, in a very hopeful way, tending to sleep offers such rich opportunities—for attentiveness, performance, mental health, and well-being.

What you don't do

Procrastivity. Pseudo-work. Fake- or make-work.

These drain, distract, and disillusion. There's no actual work getting done. Yet they're deliciously sneaky—procrastivity makes it seem like work's getting done, meanwhile the *real* work is actually getting procrastinated further away. What am I talking about?

Spending time doing things that *are* actually useful, just doing them *instead* of the deep, complex, generative schoolwork that needs doing.

Imagine that your learner has a critical book review due in two days, they've just wrapped up the book, they haven't *exactly* started. They also have a messy room. They also love to bake healthy snacks. They also have a family responsibility of walking the dog.

With the deadline looming, along with a little bit of overwhelm as the minutes tick on, focus is fading. What might they choose? To clean their room. To do some healthy baking. To walk the dog. All lovely, all helpful, all thoughtful, all necessary.

Just not right now.

It's procrastinating on things that feel like work yet aren't.

Emptying the dishwasher, taking out the recycling, folding the laundry.

All helpful.

All aren't the book review.

And what happens to our already faded focus? More fading. We're still using up that brain-power, still drawing on cognitive resources, the day and energy are still passing. The result? That book review is even further away, it's even harder to concentrate, and the procrastination, and that overwhelm, has taken further hold.

So, what *not* to do? The things that aren't really work when a learner actually has to do work. Especially if paying attention and *keeping* attention are a challenge. Procrastivity is just making it worse.

Raising focused learners

Lots is lost when attention slides.

It's not that distraction is unilaterally "bad." A friend might've spontaneously popped by, or a text might come through from a loved one, or a new pet might be welcomed to the family, or a creative pursuit might vie for attention.

The tricky part is if distractedness is frequent because it takes more work and costs learners.

Things take longer which means less time for replenishment —and space to do the outside-of-school things they love to do. Distractedness, in other words, is its own kind of inefficiency.

Efficiency isn't everything; we're not machines. I don't label myself a "productivity expert" despite supporting productivity strategies. I prefer being known as a non-toxic productivity and attention-restoration expert, a guide, or more like a friend.

A friend to learners, helping them cultivate or renourish capacity to pay attention, to produce well, and to be efficient with their efforts, at least some (or more) of the time, so that there are more minutes for them to spend the way they wish.

Learning strategies are the truest friends to learners.

In many ways, learning strategies, like those around focus, are about freedom. Freer thinking, instead of spent on concern over work. Freer tests, instead of being dreaded. Freer heart-space, instead of feeling ashamed about or "not good at" school. Freer minutes—because a learner had more alertness, and clear, strategic ways of working on school tasks—to live their lives.

What has me forever-riveted is how to help make things "better"—lighter, less stressful, more interesting, more doable for learners to support their own leaning in—when it's not so easy to feel motivated.

When a learner is checked out and says with words or body language that they don't care much about their class (or course) (or program) (or teacher), I want parents and families and community carers to have things to say and, if there's openness, to suggest.

Chapter 6

Taking the Plunge to Being All-In

Boredom, listlessness, restlessness, apathy, and even demotivation can affect our kids profoundly. These states of low energy can be overwhelming for learners, making them feel stuck and purposeless. The work they need to complete feels increasingly further away and unachievable.

These feelings often strike at the least "convenient" moments—like when an exam is approaching, or a big project is due.

Learners will often describe the situation as, "I can do things I'm interested in." The challenge lies in when something isn't naturally compelling.

One risk is that the student turns this into an inward judgment—like there's something wrong with them. Like their lack of interest in a particular lesson, task, or project is a "problem." With this, there can be that sneaking shame.

Like any challenging experience of a learner, or any interaction between parent and child, it never comes to any good to say, "snap out of it." Nor does "just get started" or "just move on with things" or "just do it" ever truly work. Instead, sharp demands of these kinds, understandably spoken in frustration by a worried parent, lead to deepening a student's stuckness, and their potential shame over it *not* being easier.

A learner wants school (and life) to be easier. They want to feel interested. The want to like their classes and teachers, want to be able to understand and do the work, want to struggle, stress, and suffer less. No student—no *person*—enjoys feeling out of place, out of sync, or out of step. Your learner would rather be captivated by and feel capable of doing the academic tasks in front of them.

Luckily, we can nudge them, shift the energy, and make significant change through learning strategies.

Boredom is a feeling

The first step to getting our kids out of their rut, re-engaged, and motivated again is to find ways to help them language what it is they're feeling. *And* to name that, indeed, boredom, ennui, frustration, and listlessness *are* feelings.

And, because they're feelings, it means that they will pass.

I'm not diminishing feelings, how strong they can become, how uncomfortable they can feel. Indeed, there are such potent emotions, we can wind up feeling like the ground will give way or the sky will swallow us whole—the key thing is that...they won't. Even heart-wrenching feelings like despair, anguish, sorrow, as here-to-stay as they might seem, as heavy and immovable as they might be experienced, they don't stay.

Why is this important?

Boredom feels yucky, sucking away vitality and joy. It slows time down in a bad way, unlike when we're in flow. But it does pass, always.

Acknowledging your learner's discomfort, being with them, and honouring their feelings is crucial. Then, providing a clear understanding that boredom is temporary, a passing sensation, is important. It's not about downplaying their experience but offering relief by knowing it won't last forever.

The gift of not wanting to.

You're not going to barge into your learner's room and *lead* with, "your boredom is actually an opportunity!" (Although it would be kind of fun to see what response you'd get from your learner.) But their boredom *is* an opportunity. *Not wanting to* is a gift.

How so?

When your kid(s) were younger (or perhaps this is still the case for them), did they ever ask for snacks...every two minutes?

That sure happened around here. I would plan it just right before a road trip: we'd have a hearty breakfast, finishing up packing, have a substantial lunch, and *right* after, hit the road. And yet...invariably, 5 to 15 minutes into the journey, "Mom, I'm hungry!"

While I respect their hunger cues and steer clear of the food- and body-shaming I grew up with, I also gently remind them that it's okay to feel a bit hungry between meals. I've tried to teach them to sit with that discomfort without fear. And you know what? They often forget about being hungry after a while. In a world of convenience, where we can easily turn on the AC when it's hot or turn up the thermostat when it's cold, we're not always practised at handling discomfort. It's important to remember how fortunate we are if we have never truly experienced real hunger.

What's challenged by so much convenience and always-comfort that pervades this time and context—although I'm not making the assumption that everyone reading this lives a life of comfort—is that we're often under-practised at *being with* what's unpleasant.

We want bad feelings to go away (immediately). We want no conflict (with anyone). We want zero pain (ever).

We all know that that's not how it works.

Feeling bored *is* an opportunity to feel discomfort—of a low-ish stakes, less-ish painful sort. It's an opportunity to notice and tend to our habits, our go-tos, our internal storylines, our mindsets, our attitudes, our behaviours when we encounter discomfort.

If we make everything *unboring* for our learners, if they're entertained or engrossed in every moment, then they don't develop the skills of facing that emotion. If every time our child says, "I'm bored," and we pop on a riveting show, they don't have to *deal with* the discomfort of boredom.

Boredom will pass, but until it does, it's annoying, agitating, or even agonising. But it won't hurt, it won't cause harm, and it *will* help. It'll help build the muscles of: what do I do when I'm bored, how do I cope with my own boredom, and how do I do the thing(s) I need to do even if I'm not interested in them?

We can all admit as parents (even though it doesn't feel so nice to), that aspects of parenting are boring. We adore our kids, we are present to them, we cherish them. But sometimes, whether in the earliest baby days, or on *another* walk, or reading the same bedtime story for the 35th time (that week), you might've had a feeling or two of boredom.

As a professional, I guarantee there's been *at least* one meeting in your whole career that you felt bored by.

What we learn by facing boredom is that it won't hurt us, it's temporary, it's not scary, and it will never go away.

We'll never be free of boring things, boring people, boring events, boring tasks. If we try to avoid boringness altogether, making it seem like there's a "problem" when something is boring, feel like we have to "fix" ourselves or the situation, we miss out.

Instead, *lean into* the boringness. Feel the invitation to develop that being-with-boring toolbox. That releasing-to-temporary-discomfort.

Boring isn't all bad. In fact, it isn't bad at all.

Boredom busting

You might be thinking that "sitting with your boredom and its discomforts" sounds good in theory but challenging in reality. Your learner might indeed be bored, and you might agree that this temporary discomfort holds some value. Yet, you're probably wondering, "Okay, but how do I motivate them to do their work?"

As parents, our frequent next-step when our kids articulate (or straight-up whine) when something is boring is to provide something *unboring* for them to do. A distraction, a look-over-here-so-you-don't-feel-bad, a redirect. Doing anything but the thing. Hoping that doing something fun instead will coax a learner to get back into it. Like maybe if we bookend the boring thing with fun things, it'll make it easier. Hoping that doing unboring before and after will enable moving through the boring. These things are all still avoidance.

But it turns out that the most helpful strategy is the opposite.

One poignantly effective approach to getting un-bored is not to do something avoidantly fun prior, but instead to do something *more* difficult than the task that the learner is feeling unmotivated, uninspired, and uninterested in doing. In order to turn the page on boredom is to do something harder.

Isn't that mind-blowing?

Do something worse, then the bad won't seem so bad. This is mindset, but it's also dopamine. It's physiological. It also, bit by bit, seed-plants resourcing and resilience for a learner. If a student is bored and goes straight for the un-boring, this is feedback that the learner does not yet have a rich toolbox of tools for discomfort.

Now, there are some details about doing this that are essential to its success as a boredom-busting strategy. The first is that the harder task has to actually be harder.

What do I mean?

I mean, it can't be taking that shower that your kiddo has put off since yesterday. It can't be spending an hour cleaning their room that they have put off since last month. It can't be a "hard" videogame level or practising that "hard" song on guitar. It must *actually* be harder than the boring task. That's how to kick motivation into high gear—body, mind, and spirit.

For example, a learner has a 1500-word paper to write. It's not that this is a universally boring task—some learners love to write. But in this instance, imagine that the learner we're picturing doesn't love writing or hasn't found delight in this class or doesn't feel rapport with their teacher etc. And most of all, they're feeling disinclined to start or work through it and say they're feeling "bored."

If they're not able to turn to another get-started strategy—like task initiation by way of a Time Timer, a set amount of time to begin with, breaking the task down into smaller sub-tasks, internal motivation to clear this task, a reward of any kind like visiting with a friend after a writing session, or any other learning strategy you've picked up here along the way—a parent could ask them, what's an even more challenging task than this?

A great one could be studying.

Studying can be the epitome of boring. It's quiet. It's deep-thinking. It's recall-practice. And, it's full of anticipation for something usually unappealing—a test. Studying also has some usual pitfalls that add to the boringness—like that it's often left undefined and unboundaried, like knowing when a study session ends, so there can be an endless quality to it.

The boring, harder task can be not school-related, too. It can be physical. Like, if your learner hates running and finds it uninspiring, unenjoyable, and uninteresting, then they can go for a 10-to-20-minute jog—with sprints. Those sprints up the challenge.

I think you're seeing the heart of the strategy.

We're going after difficulty and complexity on purpose, such that the 1500-word paper becomes not so boringly hard to start.

Doing hard things, which boringness *can* truly feel like, is not only possible for every learner, but will also never go away. So practising new and effective go-tos is essential.

Next time your learner says, "I'm bored," you can respond, "Great! How can we make it worse?" No not like that. But you can ask, what's something that's a little bit harder, and let's begin with that.

Rethinking the ask

Sometimes, when a learner has a boring task, all kinds of story-telling will surround it. You might hear them say, "it's not actually that hard, I can start it later." Or, "it won't really take that long."

Notice when your learner does this. Actually, we can, as parents and professionals, notice when *we* do this too.

It's common and totally normal to deceive ourselves by labeling something as easy, simple, quick, or effortless; however, in reality, the task turns out to be difficult, complex, time-consuming, and demanding. It's like if we say it won't be so bad, then it won't be.

And it's not that it's bad. Hard isn't bad. Complex isn't bad. But it *feels* like it'll be bad when we are anticipating what's to come. When we're at the start of a project or task we *really* don't want to do.

Just like for our kids. It feels bad to imagine how hard something will be. How unpleasant it will feel to sit there thinking, writing, practising—instead of all the fun, *very* pleasant things we could be doing instead.

There's really something in that *before*. In that just-prior, anticipatory place. Where we're looking ahead at that 1500-word paper, that studying, with dread.

So, what a more natural thing to do than, to justify our putting off starting a little longer, to characterise the work as *not* so bad. That it won't take long. So, therefore, the learner won't need the full time to do it. Therefore, that smaller window of time can be pushed back a little. Since it won't take that much time, no problem to start a little later.

Except.

It almost always takes "that" long and is "that" hard. The problem was with our estimation, foresight, and more accurately, our self-deception.

What then is a different starting place in all of this avoidance, aversion, and articulating the paradoxical ease of the hard task?

It's to rethink what the ask really is that underlies the assignment.

Again, the key to strategies is not that one single intervention will work for every learner, or for every assignment being avoided. Rather, the hope is to equip parents—of every learner, every learning experience, every learning profile—with options, things to try, approaches to experiment with, hacks to offer.

How does rethinking the ask play out with a learner who is bored and really "not feeling it" in terms of that 1500-word essay, studying, physics lab, or any other boring schoolwork task?

At times, the learner becomes hyper-focused on the assignment, fixating on its mechanics, logistics, and minutiae.

But *underneath* these are more heartfelt asks and opportunities.

When a learner is asked to write a 1500-word paper, there are several unspoken-of aspects at play. Learnings underneath the words and the information.

One layer below this assignment is the practice of critical thinking. Of a learner being asked for their opinion and being asked to back it up. This is huge! It's an invitation for a student to take up space, and that doesn't happen very often. It's an opportunity to offer a new idea and put it in their own words. If we see the essay as a boring task of writing 1500 words, it's tedious. If the task is actually a chance to come up with a new thought, try out new wordings, and put on paper something of one's self, maybe it's a little less boring.

Let's go one layer below that. A 1500-word paper, underneath the critical thinking, is actually project management in disguise. And *that* is a skill that your learner will get to use repeatedly in their own professional lives. So, we can make that connection for them. For example, when they're a record producer and are at the start of working with a new artist on a new album, that's project management—when is the hoped-for release date, how many songs need to be recorded, working back from that when do the songs need to be written, polished, and arranged. Now that essay is fodder for a passionate career-journey.

Mischaracterising the difficulty, time, and effort takes us further off course. It never changes the *actual* difficulty, the *actual* time needed, the *actual* effort. But, instead of moving further away from the task, we can go underneath it.

We can rethink, reconsider, and reposition what are the *actual* opportunities that belie the seemingly straightforward, and boring, task.

Raising less bored learners

I'm hopeful that there's a strategy or two, or reconceptualised approach, that lands as helpful, for you and your learner.

Boredom isn't scary, but it's unpleasant. It won't swallow us whole, but it's challenging to sit with. It's all about our relationship to boredom.

My go-to as a parent and learning strategist is to hold both the individual learner and particular context alongside the larger life implications. They co-exist. As in, in *this* singular moment where my learner is absolutely flat-out bored, I want their boredom to go away for them. I don't want my kiddo, or anyone else's, to suffer. I want all learners to feel curious. To feel rapt by what they're learning, listening to, and doing. To feel inspired by the lesson or work in front of them. To feel all-in.

And yet.

I know that's not possible. And that there's important work to be done when a task is boring—that isn't just the schoolwork itself.

It's in how we accept boredom, release our tension around it, relate to it, and *try* to do the work anyways.

As parents, we can soothe a learner's boredom in this moment and in the future when it arises. But, instead, we could also help them build a repertoire all their own of strategies to lean on instead. So that their boredom doesn't overtake their commitments, the opportunities for deeper, underneath learning, or their well-being.

No learner can be all-in all the time, but we can support them in *leaning into* their learning, instead of running the other way.

PART THREE

GETTING THROUGH IT— HOW TO ENCOURAGE KEEPING ON GOING

You know what is sure to backfire? Saying to your kid, "Just do it."

Sorry, Nike.

Ever said that? What happened next?

Same goes for "just start," and for sure, "just get it done."

For many learners, that "just" feels miles away. Not to mention shaming and devoid of heartfelt understanding.

In that same vein, platitudes over perseverance also fall flat, or even hurt. Keeping-on-going is marvelous when it happens. But it's punishing when it doesn't. When something, or many things, are in our learners' way.

Often, *too* often, perseverance support comes in by way of language—and fear—around "quitting." "Don't quit." "Never give up." And, as we started, "just do it" (or "just get on with it").

To be sure, there are many times where our learners, like all humans, underestimate themselves, presuppose failure, or were conditioned to believe that they'll never "make it" or succeed. This chapter will focus on strategies for how to get through what we want and most desire to get through and how to reach our heartfelt aims and commitments.

It feels necessary to say that sometimes quitting is the best choice.

In part, the word "quit" holds so much weight, and so much judgment. If we softened the edges of this word, or saw it in a new light, it's no different than "letting go," "pausing," "changing direction," or "waking up." There are so many reasons to quit, or *not* persevere, or to *not* keep going, whatever we wish to call it.

103

Some reasons have to do with harm and safety. Some have to do with injustices. Some have to do with life context, like the unexpected hurts and hurdles our families experience. These can all be very good reasons to stop, rest, or regroup.

Other reasons have to do with interests—they change, and that's okay. Or to do with values-alignment—these can get clearer, and that's wonderful. Or to do with opportunity—these can emerge, and that's magical.

What I'm trying to do is take the sting out of "quit," and trying to name good reasons to persevere and good reasons to *not*.

My aim is to offer keep-going strategies *if* keeping-on-going feels like the right, healthiest, most worthwhile, most honest, most awake thing to do.

How can we know?

That's going to depend on how your learner, and your family, decision-make. A personal, braided combination of belief, pro-and-con list-making, gut-based intuition, wise counsel, spirit-whispers, prayer, or time.

Chapter 7

Hardening Habits of Ease

We're all bombarded with discussions, ever changing information, and advice on habits, whether as parents or professionals. The abundance of content on routines and good and bad habits can feel overwhelming. Sorting through it all, making sense of it, and figuring out how to apply it effectively for learners, especially concerning academic performance and well-being, can be challenging. Despite all of this noise, habits remain crucial to consider.

What are habits about?

Habits make things easier.

What things?

Mornings, keeping house, paying bills. Getting stuff done, anything and everything. *All* things. Habits make *life* easier.

How?

Without habits, everything would need conscious, active thinking and consideration. We'd need to weigh out each decision. It's not that thinking is bad, and it's not that careful consideration should be done away with. It's that if e-v-e-r-y encounter, wondering, possibility, and option required intentional focus, time, and brainpower, we'd be exhausted. Likely before 9am.

Habits make for automation in the best possible way, specifically automation of the things that *can* be automated. Habits are the rhythms, the workflows. They're the established choreography, particularly with the little things that make up the day-to-day like dressing and grooming and aspects that we don't need to spend a lot of energy on. Without habits, the cost would be too high.

Sometimes, our habits or habitual behaviours don't serve us well. Late-night snacking, choosing caffeine over rest, neglecting posture when using devices (not to mention smoking or excessive behaviors leading to addiction, though not the focus here) warrant reflection.

Habits help. We're less depleted because of them. But with all the information and disinformation about habits, it can be hard to decipher what's the best support for learners on their school paths.

We'll focus on what works, what doesn't, how healthy learning habits get made, and how to dissolve unhelpful work habits.

A starting place

Where to begin?

With a book full of strategies, and a life full of hopes, it can feel difficult to know where to begin. Should we start with a new habit, or begin by breaking one? And *which* one?

I'm oriented around ease, and around things that feel uplifting, so my approach is to start with building a habit anew, and around something that feels like not just doable to bring consistency to, but that it will have rewarding impacts.

Like what?

Two starting places that can have immediate and transformative results are sleep and studying.

Let's start with sleep and keep it simple.

First, have your learner name what's not working for them about sleep. This can be quick, but make sure they're honest. Is it an everyday, always-exhaustion? Is it an out-of-syncness with family and friends, keeping opposite hours? Is it about getting continuously sick? Is it about mental health repercussions?

Second, understand the frame. A close colleague and long-time collaborator made me realise years ago that I had my work-sleep rhythm backwards, and that my miscalibration was leading to daily fatigue.

I was an emerging professional, I was in grad school, I was a parent to a wee one, so it made *some* sense what I'd been doing. At that point in my life, I would work until I was done the work. I would stay up a little to get a paper done. I would stay up a little more to get the meals prepped for the next day. I would stay up a little more to get some basic house-tidying done. And, when I felt I *could* go to sleep—when I'd done enough—that's when I would.

And yet, the alarm clock was always set for the same time. It's not like I could shift my schedule in the morning. I would borrow from my sleep and depending on how much, I wouldn't get enough.

I'd wake up *so* groggy. I was nowhere near ready to wake on my own—I needed deep sleep.

I was in a habit of sleeping around my work—when I was finished, that was bedtime.

What my colleague shared about her sleep priorities, and that she practised the inverse. She had a fixed window, let's say 9pm to 7am, that was set in stone. She would never borrow from sleep to do work. She boundaried her work to her true waking hours and left her sleep window untouched.

Now, if there was a friend gathering, a special dinner, or an event, of course she would go! It's not that her sleep window was rigid to the exclusion of joy. And, if there was a *major* work event once every year or two, then sure, she might be more flexible with that window.

But on the day-to-day, her commitment to sleep was a firm, healthful habit, and work needed to flex around it, not the other way around.

What will your child's frame be? Have your learner pick a bedtime that's realistic. If they've been going to bed at 3am, then having them all of the sudden starting winding down at 10pm might be too drastic a switch. There might need to be a transition period of slowly bringing that 3am more in alignment with their desired habit.

Third, plot the order. What's the sequence going to be? If the desired sleep window is 10pm to 8am, then we need to consider what happens *before* 10pm to make that a reality. And, if 8am is wake-up and school starts at 9am, what is the order of things in that time?

For the bedtime habit, encourage your learner to consider:

- how long it takes them to fall asleep.
- what winds them up and what calms them down.
- what they can do prior to going to bed that will support getting going in the morning.
- and, perhaps most importantly, before bedtime, what helps transition from the work, stress, to-dos of the day, and feels restorative and nourishing.

If 10pm is bed, and if it takes them a half hour for teeth-brushing and grooming, then we need to factor in before that some time to decelerate from the day. What feeds your kid's soul? Is it journaling, reading sci-fi, sketching, music-playing? And prior to that, is there a family TV show?

A new bedtime habit might look like this if you eat dinner at 6:30pm:

- A short, after-dinner dog-walk or stroll around the neighborhood.
- 7pm ish 1 hour of schoolwork (maybe split up into 2 half-hour sessions, like Pomodoros of 25 minutes on and 5 minutes off).
- 8pm ish 1 hour of family, play, connection time.
- 9pm ish 1 hour to physically get ready for bed, engage in something quiet, screen-free, gently creative or contemplative.
- 10pm bed.

I'm not suggesting rigidity, but a scaffolding for a new rhythm, especially if your learner has been working until at least 11pm most nights.

Where does that worktime go that's "lost?" Well, back to time management, prioritising, and planning. That late night work is usually the result of daytime procrastination. Not always, but mostly. And I'm not judging that. I understand why procrastination happens—there are so many reasons. But, my perspective from the last ten years of having flipped and committed to a sleep-first schedule is that procrastination will be less, efficiency will be more, and quality of life will be *much* more, if you're well-rested.

And well-restedness, even in our super busy lives, *is* possible.

Now, take studying. That's another good place to start.

Studying, whether for a low-stakes book quiz or a weighty final exam, often gets avoided, delayed, started late, and done inefficiently. It's *not* students' fault; they're rarely shown how to study—I've covered this extensively elsewhere, so I won't dwell on it here.

What do students most often do? Re-write their notes from class, skim slide decks, re-read chapters.

What *should* students do? (And I say "should" with a bit of reservation because I'm a nudger and a motivator *not* a should-er.) But, if a student is experiencing wobbly confidence in tests, high anxiety about them, and poor marks, then that's a learning strategy problem *not* a student problem.

Instead of any of those wildly ineffective habits, like re-writing notes, students will experience skyrocketing comprehension, recall, and performance if they do two things: 1) practice questions and 2) practice those questions over time with space in between.

That's it.

Yet sadly, students don't know this. They're given a write-date, but not a how-to-get-there plan. They're told, "study harder," but no insight or tools into what "harder" means—for longer, with more stress? I would argue, study *easier*—more efficiently, effectively, easefully. Or, learners are told to, "make a study schedule," but without a clear directive about what to schedule—is by blocks of time, or reading, or "reviewing," and what do you actually do when you "review" anyway?

Now, because students aren't usually taught the *how* of studying, when it comes to an evening's work, that "studying" task might get jotted on a to-do list yet will more likely get triaged to the next day. Why? It's back to that how. What to do during that "studying" task window is undefined. When to start, how long to study for, and how to know when done are left unboundaried.

So, a new habit could be, at the start of each day's homework session, to begin with 10 or 20 practice questions.

Now, if your learner is in fourth year computer science, it might need 30 questions. If your learner is in grade 5 and prepping for a math quiz, it could be 5 questions.

Where do these practice questions come from? Four sources: the teacher (by way of a review package or practice exams), the texts (by way of end-of-chapter review questions), the student (by way of creating a few after each lesson and each reading), or by AI (by creating a prompt).

The habit-building that we're getting at comes with when that studying is happening, and how it's happening. You can see that a very clear way to do this is by number of questions (10 or 20, or 5 or 30). It can also be done by time (20 minutes at the start of every homework session). Or, by topic (zeroing in on one topic, formula, application, etc.). And, "studying" is no longer languishing on that to do list—it's been moved earlier on the evening's plan, if not first.

As a final thought, what would happen for your learner if they: were consistently sleeping, at a regular time, with good habits leading into bedtime, and never borrowing from rest to do homework; and, if studying was done by way of a clear number of practice questions (or minutes), done daily or every other day, as the first thing on the evening's task list?

If these were practised, consistently, they'd become the new norm. They'd become habits that would lead to a transformed school experience.

Make the path easier

Habits are all about easing constant decision-making and workflow.

There's another dimension of ease that's central to habit-formation, and that's easing the "path."

What path?

The path to firming up that habit. Of moving it from a deliberately repeated practice to just a thing you do.

What does "ease" have to do with it?

If the behaviour you're looking to become habitual is complicated to repeat, unwieldy to integrate, then turning it into that established habit can be tricky.

What do I mean?

Creating a consistent sleep routine is more challenging if your learner works shifts at erratic times, including during the night.

Creating an after-school studying routine becomes more challenging when your learner needs to accompany a sibling to irregularly scheduled sports practices.

In a nutshell, easing the path has to do with your learner setting themselves up for success.

Whether your learner's schedule is clear, open, and regular, or all over the map, whether their commitments are few or many, making the pathway easier in their intentions and attempts to repeat the action(s) they wish to become habitual can make all the difference.

The classic, often-told example of this pathway-easing is to get your exercise clothes ready and laid out at night before bed if the desired new habit is to start moving more in the morning.

What could easing the path look like around solidifying a sleep habit? To start, since we're centering this in a learner's life, they could begin by outlining three specific tasks for the evening. Rather than having an endless list, they could create a clear list of three items: something for immediate completion, something for the slightly longer term (such as preparing for a test they have in three weeks), and something that's on the horizon.

From there, they would bring definition to each. How long, how much, or for how many minutes—roughly—will each of those be given time for. You'll notice that I'm not asking, "how long will they take?" But rather, I'm defining the edge. As in, *this* is how long I am giving myself for this task.

Now, a caveat, for any number of reasons, your learner might not be able to complete their to-do in that time. This becomes a case for the approach of "little and often," taught long ago by my friend Linda Graham. Little and often is about the power of practising a bit at a time. This is helpful languaging for learners, especially those prone to overwhelm, and those who see a big project and feel unable to start. Little and often reminds that they're not doing the whole thing at once, and they don't have to understand a whole topic right away. It's about chipping away.

Why mention this? Your learner, if they experience not being able to complete something in that set time frame after school can absolutely borrow from the longer-term project times. But, hopefully, and with your clear encouragement and reflection support, they can internalise that gentle project management mantra, "little and often," so that next time, what they were hard pressed to complete tonight becomes spread out over a little bit more time. And, that their upcoming projects become approached with the mindset and planfulness of little and often.

So, in this sleep habit scenario, your learner defines those tasks—how they'll start, and how they'll know when they're done, which could look like completing the 1-page science lab report, doing 15 practice study questions for a test next week, and then writing 1 paragraph towards an essay due in a month. (If your learner is a studying-procrastinator, then they might do best studying first and "getting it over with." They'll soon experience the tremendously positive impacts of "getting it over with" on the daily or every other day by way of a handful of questions.)

Why do I suggest starting a sleep habit by outlining the evening's homework? Because by doing so, we acknowledge that this particular sleep routine revolves around prioritising sleep ahead of work. For learners, forming a sleep habit must consider the importance of homework, assignments, and preparing for assessments. Simplifying things involves asking, *what time do I have available this evening, and what specific tasks do I need to accomplish during that time?* This shift in approach—from prioritising sleep to fitting work around sleep—is essential for effective sleep habit formation.

After schoolwork times become less drifty, less overwhelming, and much clearer about what it is that will get done.

Each school item has a time window, not rigid but firm. This will also help with efficiency. When a learner knows they only have 30 minutes for a task, that endless quality is gone, and many then notice more alertness and drive. It's more motivating to know that you only have to work for a half-hour than working at something "for however long it takes."

Work will take, in many scenarios, as long as a learner gives it. It cannot and should not be the only thing in a student's life. (That might feel like a dull life for many, not to mention a recipe for burnout just a little bit down the road.)

114

In and amongst the key, planned, intentional work tasks, I'd also suggest a brief evening walk or outing like sitting on the porch, walking the dog, chatting with a friend, listening to music, or a quick round of basketball. The key is to get outside just before the sun is setting, and be in that sunset light. There's sturdy research to support this kind of light exposure helps with a solid sleep schedule.

And this kind of *thinking* is the key to change. Our evenings, *cannot*, solely be about schoolwork. Our *lives* cannot solely be about work.

Time with family or chosen family, time in leisure, time re-embodying, and time to be one's unarmoured self after a day at school—these are essential. Just as essential as schoolwork—and these actually contribute to strong academic performance. Feeling connection, feeling a sense of belonging, feeling part of a community, and feeling a larger sense of purpose—these make school, and just about everything, better.

Back to sleep!

So, we've got an after-dinner, sunset walk, we have our clearly laid out, boundaried to-dos. We've got some play time, and some buffer zone time, before going to bed.

We've eased the path into work by making the exact items clear, and the duration. We've eased the path into sleep by winding down our bodies.

Easing the path can time innumerable shapes, like setting ensuring a clean, clear desk at the end of every night so that the next day it's ready to go; whatever your learner's version of laying out the gym clothes.

A different way to phrase this notion of easing the path is, *what's getting in your learner's way of having this become a habit?* And what can they do to clarify or 'declutter', even if metaphorically, the path so they can repeat that action until it's automated?

Stack the decks

One of the most powerful habit-entrenching strategies around is called "stacking." It's logical and clever, it feels doable and even a little poetic. Best of all, it taps into what learners are *already* doing.

As an aside, amplifying what learners do well, this is about the best learning strategy there can be. It is an approach that is strengths-based—which feels so important because of how often this phrase is tossed around without clear action attached to it. This leans in and leads from what learners are doing—and there is empowerment in that.

Here's how it works: have your learner think about habits they already have. The step-by-steps they always do. Consider morning or evening routines, consider how they leave the house at the start of the day and how they re-enter at the end, consider any sequences they've developed.

Habit-stacking invites us to insert a new action—that desired habit—into an already well-established pattern. This new behavior can be placed either before, after, or somewhere within a series of actions that are already automated.

What could this look like?

Here's an example. Your family would like to start incorporating a gratitude practice. A way to uplift the family vibe, push against entitlement, and to engage in an antidote to the negativity bias we each innately have. Once the desired new behaviour is identified—practising something like recounting three moments, encounters, or happenings in each person's day that they feel touched by, happy about, or appreciative of—then look for the already set sequence to stack it with.

Perhaps your family has dinner together on Friday nights. The meal might be different, kids might scatter afterwards, but the rhythm repeats: Friday evenings always (or *almost* always) include a shared meal.

Since this doesn't require any thinking, consideration, or adjustment, it's the perfect time to stack our new habit into our routine. Since Friday fam dinner always happens—we can count on it—we can include a new behaviour—that gratitude practice.

This would now look like gathering, as usual, to eat together, but before anyone starts, each family member would share the things they're thankful for.

Habit-stacking is less about a particular *time*, but more about linking—more like *marrying*—the new behaviour with something else that always recurs. So, it's not so much, "at 10am I'll do activity X," it's more like, "after I come home from school every day, I'll go for a dog-walk." Maybe that's based on wanting to get in a little bit more movement every day, or spend more time outdoors, or have a breather and break between the school day and the evening's work.

Can you feel the simplicity? It's much harder to get a new habit going when it's not tied to anything. This way, you're turning to an anchor—your robust habit sequence—to integrate something positive and new into your life.

For a student, this could mean:

- starting each homework sit down with 10 practice study questions.
- playing guitar 10 minutes before dinner.

- walking 10 blocks in morning and/or evening light.
- doing 10 repetitions of a strength movement or stretching right after closing the laptop for the evening.

The "10" is arbitrary here; it can be any number, any amount, any *thing* your learner wants to become an entrenched part of their lives.

Wherever there's already a rhythm, have your learner pop something in prior, post, or part-way through. The new behaviour, by borrowing from your learner's strong already-habits, will become part of the sequence in no time.

Let's try this example—back to the walk-taking. Imagine that the new, desired habit that you and your learner have decided upon is for them to add a little bit more movement into their day, and to have a physical break between the school day and the evening's homework. While they do this, you both figure that your learner can walk the dog.

Next envision that the first few times your learner came home, they dropped their backpack, took off their shoes and coat, and headed to the kitchen for a snack. Oh no! Now it feels *impossible* (they say) to get dressed, pause on the snack, and head back outside.

By bringing a cue, we can help your learner remember what they desire to do—until it becomes an automated, built-in habit.

What could the cue be? Hang the leash from the door handle so that your learner sees it immediately upon coming in the door. They plop their bag down, keep their jacket on, pick up the leash, and head out the door with the pup.

The cue took the remembering out of it.

Cues are hacks for habit-building. Recalling is tough work. And any to-do list that your learner might have would, at that point in the day, be buried in their school bag. Even crafting a post-it note for your learner *might* not work, depending on how observant they are (or not).

That leash, however, packs a punch. It's the prompt and symbol of what comes next.

In time, that leash might not even have to be there—the after school, pre-snack, before homework habit.

There are countless other cues that you can work with. If you and your family want to make a habit of a boardgame night but it keeps getting forgotten in the busyness and throes of a week-night, give yourself the gift of a cue. Maybe it's a boardgame on the floor. Maybe it's a boardgame on the *dinner* table so that it goes dinner then play.

Get creative with your cues, get clear about where you place them, and have them support turning hope into habit.

How will my learner remember? How will they think to do this new not-yet-habit?

Another element that supports successful habit-making is having a cue to remind you to do the thing.

Cues can take any shape; and no matter their form, they serve one essential purpose. They get you—*cue* you—to do the thing intended.

There's a cue for every context, and every learner. The most helpful ones are clear and easeful with a quick, strong impact.

Raising an easeful learner

Your child may not always be "easy"—they could be, or they might not be, and they'll be everything in between at various stages of their life. The focus has been on creating ease through habits, not on things being easy.

Indeed, habit formation—or habit unlearning, undoing, un-ravelling—is far from easy.

But habits *do* create ease. Fewer choices, more good auto-pilot, more in-built grooves of good stuff.

Sleep, studying, and most other pressing tough stuff learners experience can be thought of in terms of reducing friction, cre-ating rhythms, and streamlining.

Your learner (and your family) can bask in a less chaotic school and home-life.

Chapter 8

Enter...Tenacity

One of the most beloved books about getting stuff done is James Clear's "Atomic Habits." In it, he talks about how small changes done consistently over time are what lead to change.

Little by little can lead to sizable shifts and big accomplishments. But this isn't the only way change happens—there are people who've created transformation through radical, about-face change.

But there is such beauty in naming that we can lead with the bits, and that the bits can add up to something big.

Small bits feel less intimidating to make a start at a project or goal. It's easier to imagine keeping consistent at and making a commitment to reaching a particular endpoint in the future, and there's a sense of increased doability.

This approach, of tackling big dreams by way of little daily actions also speaks what isn't often spoken about in terms of student support, and that's academic tenacity.

Call it doggedness, call it perseverance or persistence, call it grit. There's such potency in learning strategies to support academic tenacity—to support grittiness along the journey.

If we think of this notion of being tenacious, it's sticking with something, keeping at it over a period of time, chipping away at a goal, wanting something and not being deterred by setbacks.

On my professional journey, I had a very important work mentor who was critical of anything "grit" related. He was clear that it's not the person that needs to be tenacious so much as the system they're in—the school context—that needs to shift. Why would a student *need* to be tenacious if they had the supports and access they need?

Asking learners—or anyone—to get grittier, well, it begs some questions. Like, what does a student need grit in the face of, or to persevere through? In other words, "tenacity" comes with a caution: it's not grit at all costs, it's not "pushing through" just for its own sake, it's not sticking to something or sticking something out that's harmful and misaligned.

Where I differed from his perspective was that even though all of that's true—what students *shouldn't* have to do, put up with, or persist in the face of—I also worry about students who *want* to reach their goals, *despite* the setbacks along the way, and don't want them to feel alone and unsure of what to do when it's late at night, hours are dwindling, and panic or despair are setting in. He was talking about system change—which I'm *all* for—and I'm talking about not leaving the learner unsupported in the interim.

My intentions and practices have always been in support of students who articulated struggle. And one very common struggle would be, how do I keep going? Or, how can I get there?

SMART isn't always so smart

One of the most common how-to-get-there tools is an acronym, SMART. It's a goal-setting framework, and so curiously it's become the go-to, ubiquitous way of moving towards what one aims.

SMART emerged in the 1980's in the context of management in the business world. It was offered as a tool for clearer supervisory communication and performance review support.

- The S in SMART, in the original offering, stands for "specific." This is an invitation to be as detailed and specific as possible with the goal.
- The M is for "measurable," meaning that there's some kind of feedback or metric for determining movement towards the goal, or not.
- The A, "achievable" is about attainability of the goal and the time frame.
- The R is for "realistic," in so far as having particular goals be possible.
- And finally, T, "time-bound" is exactly that: the goal comes with an established window in which to get there.

Except.

SMART might not be so smart. Or at least not for everyone.

There have been a few shifts to SMART along the way, especially as it's been applied to learners and school settings. Specific, Measurable, and Attainable have mostly stayed the same; the T is usually "Timely," which is functionally the same; but the R is more often "Relevant" now, instead of "Realistic," which feels better rather than the accompanying shame   of something being *unrealistic* or *unreachable.*

So, "Relevant," feels little less punishing, constricting,deflating. (I might advocate for "Resonant.")

And that brings me to my larger wonderings about SMART goals: do they encourage smallness? For sure, I'm wary of anything that jumps ship from business to learning. There's enough corpo-ratisation—of process, of language, of priorities—in education. Do our go-to goal-setting models also need to be steeped in it?

What of dreamy goals? Radical goals? Out of the box goals?

What of irrelevant goals? Tangents? Missteps, ebbs in the river, and U-turns?

Questions like, where does that goal come from? (As in, is this hope born from an IG "influencer"?) What might that goal take? What worries does that goal provoke? What does envisioning realising that goal make your body feel?

These questions aren't stitched into SMART. Rather, SMART feels cold, and even a little calculating. Which, I suppose, is the point. It's meant to make a formula, in a sense, of how to get from here to there.

The conundrum as I see it is that we can only plan and plot so much. We don't know. We don't know what illness or lucky break, what roadblock or uplift, will come our way. That doesn't mean we don't *do* anything, or don't *try* for something. It just means that we can bring an awake perspective to goal-setting and what we're really trying to do—whatever the acronym may be.

Goal-setting is, maybe, about arriving at what one aims for. It's also, I would argue, at least a little bit about control. About charting a path to somewhere without knowing what's on the way.

Please don't take this as encouragement *not* to have goals. A lovely friend and mentor once said, "hope is not a plan."

It's that there might be SMARTer ways to get there.

Making a PACT with yourself

SMART isn't the only goal-setting acronym around. There are many. I'll share a couple. Not because I think we should throw away SMART, but for learners who don't vibe with it, who feel more ambitious than SMART feels like it can serve, or who are keen to try out different methods.

PACT is one of those different methods.

It's a little more current and a lot more meaningful.

P is for "Purposeful." Not so much in the spirit of "what's your 'why'?" but in the, "what's the point?" Or, "why this, why you, what's the underlying hope or vision?" Purpose in PACT is about goals with gravity.

A is for "Actionable." I wish there was a different word, but what it's really getting at is how an action or two today can help get a learner to that purposeful goal. It helps narrow the divide between the big want expressed today and the distant wish. Perhaps better put, it brings that little-bit-far-off-goal *into* the present, action by action.

C is for "Continuous." It's about *repeated* action. It's a chipping away, it's a *not* going into off-course deep dives for too long, it's a keeping-at-it.

T is for "Trackable." Whether by physical calendar or mobile tracker, noting the days, noting the attempts, and noting them over time, can be motivating. (And clarifying when we take too many days off and *not* being "continuous" with our PACT goals.)

PACT-advocates like to say, "it's like making a PACT with yourself."

Whether or not you're into cutesiness, there are some standouts: bringing meaningfulness and motivation into the picture by way of "Purposeful," and mentioning trackability can be of support, too.

Luckily, we immersed in "boredom" and motivation in the prior chapter, so we've tended to the "what if my learner struggles to *stay* continuous" aspect.

Ultimately, like any method, mantra, or matrix, if it feels resonant, if it feels helpful, then try it! It could be the tool that helps your learner on their way to reaching those big, beautiful goals.

WOOP it up!

One poignant element of goal-setting, whatever the 'system' used, is the interwoven element of problem-solving.

Such a key element? How to get from here (now) to there (what I dream of)? What do I do if I: feel like I can't on some days, don't have the budget, can't find the right mentor, ...? Indeed, the "what do I do if..." is a hugely rich part of goal-setting.

The WOOP technique gets that.

WOOP stands for Wish, Outcome, Obstacle, and Plan. It's premised on the problem-solving nature of goal-setting and invites students to contemplate and pre-plan for some of the hurdles they'll potentially face, both internal and external. Obstacles, roadblocks, barriers, dead-ends—these are named from the outset. And this helps when the challenges *not* foreseen are encountered.

The premise of WOOP is what's called "mental contrasting" where we hold both the vision of the biggest, dreamiest picture of what we want alongside the deep worry and negativity that it's impossible. And from there, cultivating an if-then plan.

How does this play out?

If we only think about the desired thing, experience, or state—that end of the goal—this alone won't get us there. Even if we put pictures up, fantasise about it, these aren't enough. We won't reach it.

Conversely, if we *really* want something yet believe we can't have it; if we're stuck in negativity, and certainty about our wish being an impossibility, we also won't reach it.

This contrast leads to a third possibility: WOOP. WOOP's mental contrasting model helps us avoid both overcommitting and under-committing. It guides us away from making assumptions and thinking in extremes of yes or no. Instead, it helps us in finding a middle ground and evaluating what the actions *would be* to reach our desired goal.

In WOOP, learners start with articulating a Wish in the form of a purposeful, ambitious aim. Then, they move to the Outcome, and detail the feelings associated with reaching that wish, imagining the best possible turnout. From there, Obstacle invites thinking through and naming what might get in the way of reaching that goal, prioritising internal factors. Finally, students create a Plan that lists If-Then; learners outline, "If (hur-dle), then I will (what positive action will be tried /taken)."

The idea is that we can arrive at success by way of moving from a heartfelt wish to picturing in full vividness what it would be like to achieve, then into what roadblocks are likely to come up, particularly inner ones like procrastination or limiting beliefs, and then into crafting clear back-up or workaround plans.

WOOP brings in heart, honours doubt, and plans for the ruts and loops we find ourselves in.

Other lovely elements of WOOP are in the process you'll lead your learner through, things like:

- When at the W stage and asking them about their juicy wish; if they don't know, it can be an invitation to have them really feel into their body and notice what makes their heart leap, the corners of their mouth lift, their eyes sparkle.

127

- When at the O stage and asking them about what it could feel like; this is an opportunity for them to practice their independence, articulating a next step or life goal that would make them happy, and to bravely dream into it, and all what it would feel to get there.
- When at the second O stage and inquiring about obstacles; this is an opening to talk about challenges yet still stay calm and regulated, an honest moment to share the stuck or fearful places.
- When at the P; this is a wonderful window to share a true coping and learning and life strategy, namely thinking through and pre-problem-solving for the challenges that will inevitably arise.

See what happens with WOOP, particularly if SMART is already in your wheelhouse, or if it's not quite done the trick or led to action and goal-reaching.

An acronym for each day of the week

SMART and WOOP are but two of many. And acronyms have such power in them—they may seem overly simple, but a part of their design is that they're easy to remember.

Researchers note that our minds can only hold four or five distinct pieces of information at a time. As in, if you gave a running list of 30 new items to learn and remember, we might only be able to recall a small handful. One of the key workarounds is to craft a mnemonic device. This is a critical, fun, and wildly effective element of studying. Giving our brains *something* to hold onto in terms of quick access to ready recall.

How do acronyms help? Think of learning the notes on a staff—and perhaps a funny phrase comes to mind, like All Good Boys Deserve to Eat Fudge. Think of the cardinal directions— perhaps you're reading the NEWS, as in North, East, West, South. Think of the biological classifications—Dear King Philip Came Over For Good Soup. Or, My Very Easy Method Just Speeds Up Naming (Planets) for, well, the planets.

Each of these turn multiple items into a single phrase. Now, instead of the 8 planets to remember, for example, there's only one phrase standing in its place.

Acronyms helps with recall, and they make it simpler for a learner to understand what steps they need to take to reach a goal without having to think too much.

Some additional goal-setting, tenacity-supporting acronyms include:

- The MoSCoW Method
Born out of the business world, specifically tech and product development, this approach has us identify, in terms of priorities, our Must-haves, Should-haves, Could-haves, and Won't-haves (aka not-right-now haves) (or, sometimes called Wished-for haves). A must-have is a non-negotiable; it's what must be done. A should-have, when planning how to spend one's time, is about important to-dos and value-adds, yet that aren't actually make or break. A could-have would be lovely, but won't hold anything back or cause harm by not tending to. And, a won't-have, in whatever iteration, is about identifying tasks or wants that just aren't priorities towards reaching that articulated goal.
- WISE Goals

At the heart of this goal-setting method is supporting big vision with key questions. The W is for Written: is the aim jotted down on paper? The I is for Integrated: is the aim in support of a heartfelt, meaningful journey, wish, or purpose? The S is for Synergistic: are the steps and micro-goals along the way congruent and aligned, or working against each other? The E is for Expansive: is this experience leading to further developing and growing? This is visionary-style goal-setting, great for dreamers, purpose-fuelled, change-maker learners. Ones who, perhaps resonate more with the big picture as kindling for tenacity rather than mini-scaffolds.

The list goes on: Stretch goals, HARD goals, and the PACT prioritisation method. There is no one-size-fits-all momentum and perseverance method. And, it's ultimately the spirit behind any model that's the key.

What's the energy behind it: in the weeds and details, or in the clouds? Both can be great—how does your learner feel? What's the underlying principle: small steps to get there, or big dreams that pull you there? What's the system at play: checking off, noting down, tracking, feedback check-ins?

Whatever the letters, it's the feel, the vibe, the underlying spark.

Even "grit" itself has a tenacious acronym: gumption, resilience, integrity, and tenacity. Not much in the way of direction to follow or scaffolded support housed within it, but a fun reminder of what grit means and comprises.

Better than any already-out-there acronym is to have your learner try making their own! Create something unique together—have them identify what would best draw out an aim worth sticking to, and how to move towards it. It could be silly, it could be straightforward, but whatever the word outcome, a self-styled acronym is personal, and potentially much more fulfilling and motivating.

An ecosystem

I'll share one more model that I've made up myself. It's a bit messy but heartfelt and in response to the rigidity of most other goal-setting schemas or productivity techniques.

In this approach to centering a goal—something to be tenacious about—you can bring to mind the notion of an ecosystem.

In an ecosystem, the pieces fit together, the parts work in synergy, and there is an all-relatedness. Everything is intertwined. I can appreciate the wholism and integratedness, and too often I hear goal-setting talked about and designed in ways that is contextless. As if sickness doesn't happen. As if there aren't system barriers, or injuries, of body and spirit. And, as if we're just individuals with each our own goals.

But, we're not. We're in communities—families, chosen families, school and work places, spiritual and activism spaces, physical and virtual, neighbourhoods and regions. We're also not simply 'free' to goal-pursue as if nothing else is going on.

In an ecosystem model, everything is part of each other; our goal is interlinked and intersupported by our surroundings.

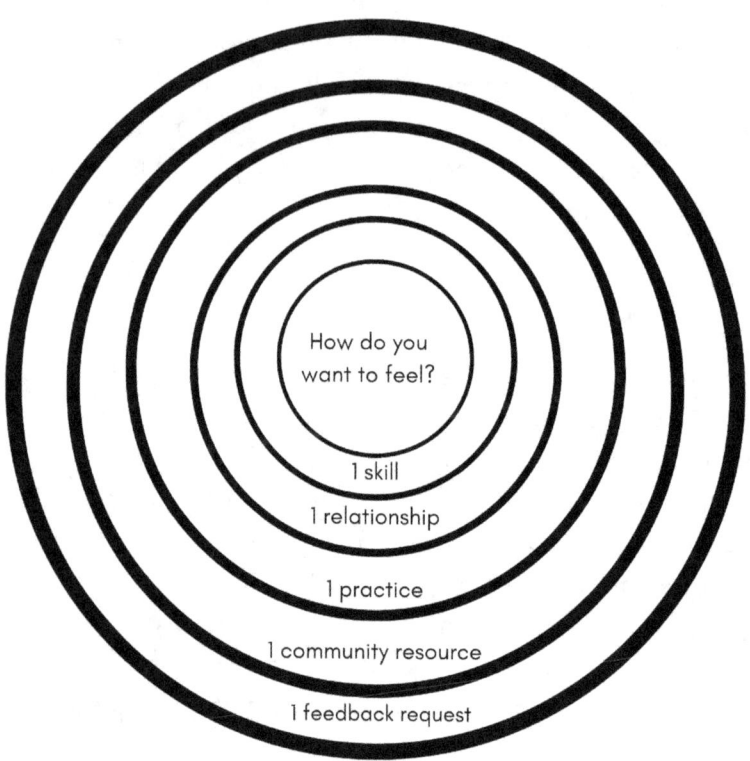

Let's try it:

- Ask your learner to depict a full-hearted goal in whatever way they feel drawn to—whether by way of words or pictures—and place that goal in the centre of a piece of paper.

- The goal is not a thing, not a place, but rather a *feeling*; ask your learner, "how do you want to *feel*?" This could be something like, "by the end of the semester, how do you want to feel?" Or, picture yourself in your first class in the first semester, or in the middle somewhere, or at graduation walking across the dais, "how do you want to feel?" This places the emphasis on the process and on the experience, rather than an arrival to or an acquiring of something.

- Draw a circle around that goal—a circle just big enough to surround the word or image.
- Outside of that circle, one level out, have your learner place 1 skill that they see needs tending to or (re)building in order to support moving towards that intended feeling. These could be skills like time management or studying, skills like deep and focused listening or professional communication; something that through bolstering would support nearing that feeling.
- Draw a circle around that skill—again, just big enough to enclose that layer.
- In this next layer out, have your learner identify 1 relationship that they could tend to in support of their aimed-for feeling. Not as in "networking," not "to leverage." But rather, as a support, or as a rallier, or as a mentor. A relationship to give to, not to get something out of per se. It's a relationship that your learner can turn to for good, reciprocal guidance and care.
- Draw another circle.
- Out from here, invite your learner to choose 1 practice that will support them on your goal-journey. It could be in direct support, like practising showing up to *everything*, 10 minutes early as a practice of punctuality; or, it could be a more traditionally spiritual activity, like breathwork, prayer, meditation, or another contemplative practice; or, it could be an energising movement practice, the

133

practise of being more timely in responding to requests, the practise of courtesy or politeness. Anything goes; any practice that would encourage the feeling wished for.

- Draw another circle.
- One layer out, have your learner articulate 1 community resource they can turn to. It could be in the school or neighourhood communities; it could be in a religious or spiritual community; it could be in a creative or activist community; a sports team or shared hobby group. Any collective that feels like it supports alignment and recalibration; a second home, in a way, and by participating in which can uplift or renew.
- Draw another circle.
- From here, in the next layer, is a request for feedback—perhaps from the identified community, perhaps from the identified relationship. Wherever good, critical, affirming feedback can be sought, note that down. Checking in, being reminded of one's blindspots, these are hugely helpful, especially when we really want something and are making moves to get there. Feedback here can come in any form; and, you can give your learner different models as examples, like a personal advisory board, or an uplifting, on-your-side Board of Directors. A trusted relationship(s) that won't project, give unsolicited advice, but when asked can listen and pose thoughtful, motivating questions.
- Draw another circle.
- The habit-supporting ecosystem model can stop here. Or, it can keep going if your learner can see other areas in their life that they can turn to for support in reaching that goal feeling-state. In a sense, it's limitless. Add layers until it no longer feels helpful or necessary.

I created this model out of the soullessness I saw and felt in so many other offerings. It's not to be judgmental, I just had a longing for a different starting place (feeling) and a different series of steps (relational,practice-based,community-honouring).

The end place might wind up being the same. As in, one student, in a SMART or PACT or WOOP model, might wish to be on the Dean's List, earning consistent, high-level marks. In the eco-system model, another student might identify wanting to feel more confident when taking assessments.

By having this specific kind of academic confidence as their desired goal, the skill they'd perhaps look at is studying, and becoming more effective and efficient in their methods. In their relationships layer, they might identify a peer in class who seems to have a balanced and successful approach around taking notes, and so asks to sit with them and learn from them—be inspired by them. For their practice, this student might feel like a healthy sleep routine is something they'd like to tend to.

You can see what's beginning to happen: the learner sees that they feel more confident on assessments, a change in studying could help, so they then start to bring in new ways; then they're learning from a peer; then they're more rested, which has all kinds of powerful ripple effects on scholastic achievement.

We can keep going—the community might be a study group, or it could be indirect, like a student club or local yoga studio. All of these nourish belonging, and would amplify academic success. Finally, feedback. This could be from a teacher, TA, or professor; it could be from a friend or partner; it could be from a parent or mentor. And feedback could be how much they're noticing positive changes, or how sometimes when they see the learner studying, they're distracted by their phone and wonder what might happen if they used a helpful app to block scrolling during key work time blocks.

The end goal might be the same, it's just that the route there is a little different.

Raising tenacious learners

Acronyms are tools, not life. They are necessarily devoid of animation and vitality. As such it's especially key to ask your learner, "what keeps your goal(s) alive *for you*?" And, getting curious, "where did that goal come from?" Most importantly and above all else is, "how can I help?" That's the single most important component: loving-alongsideness.

You being in your learner's corner. You trusting their vision. You having their back. Not doing it for them. Not "propping them up" with "false confidence," or any of that kind of ugly, judgmental critical feedback. Relationship, when centred, always makes for the biggest impact, makes for the most important part of our lives.

Oftentimes, goal-setting schemas are devoid of the relational. The implication then is that we, as individuals, are in it alone, doing it alone. This is sad, and it's not true. It's the people in our lives that really *make* our lives. Very few people live life without relationships—and fair choice to those who need a retreat from others. But for the overwhelming majority, we're in households and communities, partners and chosen families, pets at home and in the natural world, neighbourhoods and extended ancestral links.

What do these goal-setting methods have to do with tenacity? How did we start there and end here? When we look to the leading global post-secondary campuses, academic tenacity is named as being our inner stuff—fortitude, resourcing, capacities, and mindsets—that fuel learners in seeing beyond the immediate moment and instead towards their longer, bigger goals. And, how to move towards those goals in the face of setbacks.

Academic tenacity is about how we get through this tough moment in order to experience what's beyond it.

Goals, when the process to them is well-supported, help us do just that.

Chapter Nine

Working with Others When You Don't Want To

"Group work."

Say those words to your learner and you will hear them groan and watch them shudder. There might be an eye roll in there too.

Hear those words from your learner and a parent might feel uneasiness around time commitments and meet-ups, about whether your learner will pull their weight or wind up doing the whole project, and you might even question what the point of the project is.

Even though they come *from* the teacher, what is that teacher likely feeling? A sense of both hope that this cool project they've devised could work as planned, but in equal or larger measure, dread in advance of all the conflicts, last-minute emails, and disorganisation soon on their way.

Group work comes...with a lot of feels. From everyone.

For something so benign on the surface, why do they provoke groans, shudders, unease, and dread?

Because at the heart it's about working with other people.

And working with others can be spectacular. *Or*, it can be spectacularly frustrating. People have different ways of working—different rhythms and internal tempos. People have different ways of showing up, both literal and energetic—late and frazzled, open and gregarious. People have different contexts that they're working—which makes for different capacities and availabilities, different understandings and priorities, different needs and different expectations.

Working *across* difference is one of the most important skills we need to learn. More important than any content area. Why is it so crucial? Unless hermit-living is the aim, we all encounter people on the daily, we all work with people, and it's not that chances are they won't all be like you or your learner, the best work emerges when they're not.

At first glance, your child might find it simpler to team up with group work partners who think and value the same things. But, that can sometimes lead to conflicts. Having some differences, dissent, and discussing ideas from various viewpoints can actually boost creativity.

When we're challenged, we have to stretch. When we're disagreed with, we need to compromise. And in this world of quick call-outs and shut-downs, being able to sit with the discomfort of disagreement is essential. We can't push away and avoid what we don't like or align with every time it emerges. We can differ, and still feel safe. We can differ, and still cope. We can differ, and still—and *especially*—create amazing projects.

Where there's difference in group work team members, there's more voices and views included, more perspective and experience that's taken into account. This leads to greater equity, access, and relevance.

I feel compelled to outline the merits of group work because of how often it's hated on. Learners often say things like, "I wish it were an independent assignment," or "teachers give group work because it's easier for them to mark."

When learners wish for non-collaborative work in place of a group project or presentation, what I really hear is the challenges of planning, of finding time to meet, of syncing up work styles and rhythms, or getting it all going. But what's lost is the *learning* how to work with others; *how* to collaborate.

I feel like how to *converse* is a good parallel. Have you had someone talk and talk at you as if they're in conversation, but are unaware of what they're actually doing?

Being talked at isn't really having a conversation. When I find myself in those situations, I feel trapped, cornered, and sometimes unsure how to escape, especially if it's someone I've known for a long time and we often see each other.

I think about those times when I'm with my kids and they start talking, and then keep going, and then *still* keep going. I give them my fullest presence—my eyes, my heart—but I also pause them every now and again and nudge them to ask a question, to take a breath, to notice they're actually in a two-person conversation. I do this non-judgmentally; if I get an apology, I remind them that there's no need, nothing to be sorry for, that they're learning.

I teach them how to be *in* conversation. *In* relationship.

Relationship isn't just a receiving, nor is it just a giving. It is a dialogue, mutuality, and reciprocity.

That's also collaboration. It doesn't rely on a single loudest leader, and fair distribution of effort and output doesn't happen instantly—it requires working through it. It's not about one fixed pace. Establishing an efficient workflow doesn't happen without discussing and resolving it.

As for the second piece of grumpy or outright disgruntled feedback a learner might utter, about the illusion of it being easier to mark and that being the impetus for the teacher assigning a team assessment, it's not. Think of it from an educator's perspective. They *know* what's to come: late night questions, tense team dynamics, requests to switch, tech glitches, uneven contributions, the list goes on.

Easier than a group work assignment is a simple-to-mark-quiz. Make no mistake. Group projects are about centering the learner and their development as a listener, as a speaker, as a contributor, as a boundary-setter, as a reconciler, as a leader, as a team-spirit-rallier, ...as a human.

The potency of group work is in the hashing it out. It is not about educator ease. It is not so much about the content of the assignment's ask. It's the art of practice of working across difference.

Now, *how* to do it?

No more slapdash

There is no more colonial, impositional, *non*-collaborative notion than "divide and conquer." And yet that's what "group" work amounts to in most cases, particularly where the skills of collaboration aren't being taught.

The frequent pattern that I've seen with students is that they:

- Have that initial grumpy, disgruntled reaction to any group work task, whether project or presentation.
- See whether they get to choose their team members or not (and if so, grab their friends ASAP).

- Identify how much it's worth (and then adjust anxiety levels to match).
- Then, after securing a topic, splitting up the work ("you do that, I'll do this").
- Slap it together at the *very* very end, —usually the 11th hour— and make it seem like it was done collaboratively.
- Throughout, even with friends, there are inflamed tensions over work unevenness, someone not showing up, someone not pulling their weight, someone being late with work.
- Also throughout, contemplation as to whether or not to tell the teacher about the team hurdles.
- And, again throughout, anger, resentment, and begrudging of the task and the teacher, putting all aspects of the group assignment down.

It's not easy.

It's not easy being a student. (Or a parent.) (Or an educator.) (Or...a person.)

Group work is a challenge and sometimes, it's full of conflict.

Yet, collaboration *is* a skill. Diving things up into separate parts is much less of one.

Working on a thing together, in different ways—across *all* of the differences—is a necessary, rich-as-can-be skill that instead of running away from by the division approach, *can* be taken on and embraced.

If we go with the centering of relationship as a key element, then let's begin there and how to do *that*. Why? In the divide and conquer version, students are beginning with the work. How to get it done as conveniently and efficiently (in some ways) as possible.

It's prioritising the end over the process of getting there; it's prioritising the product over the people working together. Yet, it doesn't have to be that way. And, I firmly believe that when you have a team working together, the work gets done in a healthier way and to a better result.

So, let's try *that*.

Relationship at /as the centre

How are relationships built?

If that's our new place from which to do group work, how do we *do* relationship?

Relationship = time + tenderness.

Relationship is about the minutes and hours spent in doing, thinking, creating, in any kind of combination of "real life" and virtual. And, relationship is about sharing—tenderness isn't about baring all, revealing TMI, dishonouring boundaries, digging for personal information or *invasiveness*. It's about being humans together. (After all, we're humans before we're "students.")

So, what does that look like? It begins with, when group members are assigned or come together, getting together to *not* do work together. See what happens when your learner starts with the team first before the tasks. (The tasks will come, not to worry.)

Be together, get less awkward together, figure out overlaps and differences, laugh a little. *Share*.

Share what? Nudge your learner to invite their group mates over. Serve a sweet, make niceties about school, then nudge them to go for a walk, shoot some hoops, or go the local playground (no matter how old these learners are). Why? Because this gets rid of discomfort of not knowing what to say right away, of nervous eye-contact, of strained silences. Have them go *do* something together!

When we focus on a relationship, a remarkable realisation happens for learners: it dismantles our certainty of *time*. In students' usual way with group work—that detesting and dividing—relationships are often seen as an impediment. They get in the way, they slow things down. People are the roadblocks to "just getting the work done."

I feel clear that the larger, underneath, and richest element of a group work assignment is that relationships *are* the work. I understand that that's a bit existential for a learner who needs to hand something in. (But between you and me, parent to parent, that's where the social-skills-unfamiliarity, social awkwardness, even social anxiety get some practice, airing out, and prioritisation.)

But *even with* that "gotta get it done" imperative, bringing a relationship-focus to the work will make for more efficiency.

It sounds counterintuitive but let me explain.

When we go straight to turning a community project into an individual one that gets plopped or pasted together at the end, there are no real relational bonds. People are objects; they're means to an end. The end being that deadline and that learner meeting unspoken, unshared expectations.

Talk about a recipe for *unmet* expectations! For people then just doing their own separate task in their own way on their own timeline according to their own individual needs without awareness, or there even being any, community needs. It's everyone for themselves, really! It's built into the design.

But if relationship is centred, there are group milestones, group processes, group norms. And these are decided *as* a group. *For* the group.

And most of all, when there's been that time spent on each other, not the 'official' work (just the deep underneath work), the bonds, trust, and respect built prevent the no-shows, the lateness, the finish line drama.

People care about people, which ripples out to caring about the work. But the inverse isn't a necessary flow—to care about the work doesn't necessarily extend to caring about the people.

Naming needs

There are so many built-in, underlying learnings below the surface of the group work task.

Again, this is the way with schoolwork. It *looks* like studying, but it's actually about prioritisation, inner-resourcing, boundarying time, and the list goes on. It *looks* like preparing and giving a presentation, but it's actually about repetition and practice, finding one's own voice, embodied confidence, somatic strategies for stress reduction, etc.

Underneath the task of group work lies the lesson of self-advocacy—of voicing one's needs aloud to others who also have needs.

What a gift!

Naming one's needs is as important as it gets. It's linked with consent—making sure we get to stand in our yesses and nos. It's linked with undoing shame—standing radiantly in our identities. The list goes on of the built-in lessons housed within school tasks and assessments.

What does it mean to name a need?

I'll give you an example from when my kids were younger, and I would be teaching large lectures—I would let them know that I had to keep my phone on and if it rang, I would check it and look to see the first three digits. This would tell me if it was my kids' school. We're a super small family, there were no extra sets of hands, so if it was a teacher or principal calling to let me know my little one was sick or injured, I needed to know, pick up, and attend to it right away.

This felt important to me to share with my students because I wasn't unintentional about the presence of my phone in class, it wasn't that my students weren't centrally important to me, it wasn't that I was distracted. I needed my phone out and available, and if I got a call, I'd need to check it. Sharing this was a way for me to feel empowered in my decision, clear and with integrity in the multiple roles and identities I inhabit and reassuring to my students and my commitment to them too.

A poignant scenario from a dear former student of mine really takes it home. I was teaching, and she would often come in late, breathless, and a bit out of sorts. When she felt like I could be trusted, she let me know that she worked night shifts and as such was often racing to our early morning course.

For her, this felt important because she didn't want to be misunderstood as disorganised, as not *trying* to make it to class, as disrespectful (not that I was understanding her these ways). She needed for me to know something of the structure of her life. Just as I needed my students to know something of the realities of mine.

I can't tell you how many students I know who hold back sharing what they need. But, it sure was a treat to hear from students, especially after *teaching* them about the importance and art of self-advocacy, about some of their need-to-knows.

I had a student share that because of her vomiting phobia, she required a seat closest to a garbage pail and the door.

I had a student share that they're a caregiver for their grand-parents, and they'd be popping in and out of class to take family and medical calls.

I had a student share that she was evicted and searching for housing, and she'd be requesting extensions for her assignments.

Students have as *real* lives as they come. If they feel safe to share even just the broadest strokes about what they need to make their real lives work, this can change everything.

What 'kind' of everything? It can lead to compassion and un-derstanding, it can lead to empathy and care, it can lead to ideas and direct support, it can lead to equity of output and deadline flexibility.

I know there's that notion of imagining oneself in the shoes of another. This is tricky because we can't be. We take our lens and our embodied experience with us wherever we go, including in our imaginations. So, instead of imagined empathy, what if we listened with our whole hearts, heard another share their needs, and then honoured them exactly as such.

I'm not sure we need to picture ourselves in the life of another; we need to hear and heed the perspective and requests *from* that life. It doesn't require me pretending to walk in their body, their experience, their worldview. I can accept and honour from my own body, experience, and worldview.

It's like the difference between the Golden Rule and the Platinum Rule. In the Golden, it's all about treating other people the way we would like to be treated. It's ultimately about what we want and need, and then transferring that onto another. Imposing it even. As if it's the same.

The Platinum Rule has us treat other people *the way they say they want to be treated.*

It's an honouring of what someone says they are and need.

I don't need to imagine what they need based upon what I require; I can just listen to them speak or share their needs.

The possibility of alchemy

One of the biggest losses in hating on group work is the missed opportunity for alchemy.

I don't mean actual turning things into gold; I mean, the extraordinary magic that can only happen when people, as inconvenient and messy as we all are, come together.

Group work and working with others can be time consuming, but what are we rushing for? What is the rushing that a student feels they need to participate in?

That zooming, sometimes frenzied quality that a student might characterise their school life by was inherited. Learners aren't making that pace, that frenetic quality. It's a societal, if not global, push for productivity. I promise not to go into a full-scale rant about pushing back against this, but it could be a wonderful conversation starter between you and your learner about:

- What is learning for?
- What, as a parent, were your most memorable moments in your learning journey?
- What has notably served you along your professional pursuits from your academic path?
- What would you do differently, if you went back?
- What was your approach as a student then, and what do you think it might be like now?
- And, what endures—what memories, skills, achievements?

I won't ever really get to know, but I would guess that most of your relived highlights, when you share them with your kiddos, are relationships. A beloved or meaningful teacher. An unexpected mentor. A friend or partner. A team or student group. It will be the *people*.

Your learner might push back and say that, somehow, all that is different from a frustrating group work project. Or, that the people they've been assigned to work with will *never* fall into that "most memorable" bucket.

Except.

We can't know.

Maybe then it becomes an opportunity for you ask your learner:

- Has there ever been anyone you've misjudged?
- Has there ever been someone you couldn't stand at first and who later became a friend?
- What has been the most unexpected relationship they've ever had?
- Who was their favourite teacher, why, and did it start out that way?

What a beautiful opening for sharing and about the misperceptions along the way. The misgivings that turned into marvelous bonds.

That's only possible when we work with others.

Raising well collaborators

The other truly remarkable thing is that working with others is where the *best* ideas come from. Outstandingly creative projects are happening all over the world—as I write this, as you read this. New designs, new technologies, new remedies, new everything— that are gripping, helpful, life-saving even. And they're only possible because of group work. That's the beginning.

Share with your learners the stories of Apple. Share stories of Outward Bound. Share stories of social movements and revolutions and fights for freedom.

It's always people.

I don't mean to inflate it. I don't mean to suggest that it will be revolutionary work your learner will be getting up to. (Although it might.)

But there's always at the least the possibility of magic, of alchemy, when we open up to the wonder of others and the opportunity to work with them.

PART FOUR

GETTING AROUND IT—HOW TO REIGNITE AND REDIRECT CREATIVE ENERGY

If you looked up, "what is the most watched TED Talk of all time," what appears? Sir Ken Robinson's 2006 talk entitled, "Do Schools Kill Creativity?" At the time of writing this book, his video has more than 76 million views.

76 million views. On schooling. And it's dulling effects.

The most watched talk isn't some big Hollywood thing. It's not flashy. It's not a video on AI. Rather, what's been most sought out and watched was an 18-minute heartfelt sharing about the potential *harms* of school.

It's on how schools, as kids age, educate learners more and more from the "waist up." Instead of dance, the focus is math; instead of drama, the focus is science. And these foci just in-tensify year after year.

Creative thinking as I'll explore here isn't relegated to "the Arts," rather cross-discipline creativity.

I'm insisting that wild and wonderful ways of thinking, doing, and being are all welcome.

So often, school systems wind up looking and feeling like, "do this," "do that," "do more of that," "do less of this." Repeat. It's often a tight, rigid, worksheet-filled process that learners are led through.

There's zero blame. It's a fraught ecosystem. It's inherited and gets perpetuated. But there are so many ways to learn, and to *be*. And these get lost, or outright quieted, along the way.

Creative modes of expression, creative problem-solving, creative responses—let's nudge our learners to bring their full selves to how they do school. I'm acutely aware that when I say this there is an enormous safety component. Learners have to feel safe at school; families have to feel safe in communities. And so many don't. So, I'm not advocating pushing our deep need for safety aside.

I'm encouraging, instead, that learners get to know what they're radiant at. That they get messy, that they experiment with all kinds of materials and approaches and modalities. That they ask their teachers if they can interpret an assignment in ways that feel aligned or *alive*.

I'm hopeful that, more and more, educators will offer more choice to students about how they can respond to assessment prompts. There is room for the poetic, the theatrical, the colourful, the design riffs.

Given that the most resonant TED Talk ever is about creativity, we'll dedicate some time in this chapter to discussing *how* to nurture creativity and empower your learner to develop into their true selves.

Chapter Ten

It's All One Big Makerspace

Too often students are told there's only one way to do school. The brochure, the recruitment videos, the promo—it all looks like school happens in a linear, start-to-finish, straight line kind of way.

As parents and educators, we know firsthand how untrue this can be.

In *Feel Good Learning*, I shared this line that an early mentor spoke that still lands so loudly and resonantly for me, "there is no one way to do university." And, really, it's broader than that, "there is no one way to do school." (Truth is, of course, that it's bigger than that still, "there's no one way to do *life*.")

But learners aren't told that. A "good" student looks like this and does X, Y, Z. Being "good" at school comes with a bunch of assumptions.

Yet, there are *so* many ways to be a good student and good at school. (And, sometimes the best decision for a learner might be to be medium-okay at school but great at life.)

If we sit with this notion, that there's no singular way to do school, I wonder how that could land for a learner who is having a tough go of finding their path or groove.

How does it feel for *you*?

Did anyone, along your own school journey, mention or suggest that to you? I can share a firm "no" for myself on this question. It wasn't that I was told outright that there was a set way of doing things, of moving along the school years, it was just assumed. It's not that it was linear or un-messy for me, but, going to school just came with expectations about how to show up, what to ask or not ask, what to reach out for help with and what not to, what parts of myself I showed or kept hidden, what of myself I shared in my work and what I didn't.

It was like an engrained way of understanding of how to be a student.

But my professional life has been in service of students for who that assumed way of doing and being *isn't* working. And, in a context where there is so much not working for so many, and more voices are being heard, so there feels like an openness to have this larger conversation.

It's no longer that a learner needs to fall into binaries of good / bad, A-student / bottom of the class, good at math and science / good at languages and arts. We can contribute to the pushing against this, and help make more space for our learners to *be* themselves.

Doing school a dozen+ ways

A dozen might be selling it short. There are *countless* ways to do school. And the more we share them, the more we normalise this, heal shame, and broaden the system.

What do I mean?

The pandemic showed *all* of us that learning can happen in different places. So much that felt new for so many became the norm.

Asynchronous, virtual learning, learning management systems, video-hosting platforms. The list goes on. The word "hybrid," in the context of school and work, is here to stay. (Maybe "hybrid" is even more the word of the year than "pivot.")

Which is—to say that technical functionality, modes of "hosting" learning spaces—there is a fluidity that will only become more elegant and seamless in the variety of ways that students can participate in learning.

But that's the simplest in terms of the myriad of ways to do school. There's so many more.

For decades really, it was either go to a school or get homeschooled. And indeed, homeschooling is not only alive and well but on the rise during and since the pandemic. It's worth noting that within homeschooling, there are also innumerable options: parent-only led, screen-free, homeschool community swaps or pods, and also specific programming designed for homeschooled learners, created with timing and social interaction in mind.

I know several homeschooled learners who also get to learn by way of the school-of-life: traveling with their parents to stay all together with relatives abroad for months at a time, learning languages and customs; on boats, learning nautical rules, ocean rhythms, and all about aquatic life. The list goes on of homeschooling permutations, from in-the-living-room to across-the-globe.

Again, this is still just the familiar.

More and more students I'm working with 1:1 are creating mosaics of their school schedules:

- One student fell in love with a subject that wasn't offered at her school, so sought out a single online version of it and took it at her regular school in a classroom that wasn't being used during that period.
- One student grew to adore a particular subject area so had a co-op placement arranged in order to assist a teacher with lab set-up and supporting younger students through experiments.
- One student had a course conflict with two required courses being offered at the very same time, so negotiated attending one of them asynchronously.

These certainly require teacher and school support. But the more we can scaffold our kids' self-advocacy, particularly when they are besotted with a subject *and* can find creative solutions, the better.

There's still more!

"Alternative" or "mainstream" schools for elementary and high school aren't the only options; learners are trying out part-time and welcoming summer credits to take care of their mental health, pursue volunteer or paid work, or have time for athletic or creative pursuits.

Having worked in higher education for so much of my career, I see students seek facilitated opportunities like Co-op, Work Integrated Learning (WIL), Experiential Education (EE), and Placements. All variations on a similar theme—the value of professional learning.

Yet, when a student talks about "taking time off" or "taking a gap year," they're often judged. I'm delighted when I hear students noticing and taking care in response to the burnout they experience with full-throttle schedules by reducing their course load. Or, when they honour their interest in participating in paid work, entrepreneurship, or interning, not "on the side" squeezed in, but as a component of their day and semester.

The interesting tension here is that sometimes we think of only one type of work as "counting." As in, students in co-op get "better" work experience than if our learner works at the local coffee shop, used music or pet store, or in retail. Yet, what better learning, regardless of context, than how to forge new relationships, navigate conflict, deal with money, keep oneself organised, show up on time, and growing what one has responsibility for.

Getting the ideas out

The above are all ways that learners are creating school schedules and pathways. The creativity of doing school. But what about doing school*work*?

Let's *especially* flex creativity there too.

This might initially take the shape of welcoming more idea-tion and brainstorming. Encourage your learner to sit in the wrestling, whether it's with a math problem, a topic for an essay, or a multi-part lab. To take a little longer to consider different starting places, workarounds, alternative solutions, and new connections.

Creative schoolwork could be about formal creative prob-lem-solving techniques like mind-mapping. Web search "free mind-mapping tools" and scores will come up. You can even narrow it to include... "for students." (And there's always post-it notes or scrap paper taped on the wall as a *very* free mind-mapping approach.)

There are online whiteboard spaces like Miro and build-your-own structure spaces like Notion (I don't have any relationship of any kind with either, just have used and appreciate the way their functionalities support creative thinking and deep-diving).

You can also teach your learner from early on the best elements of design thinking—especially around elongating the early, idea-generating stages.

Sometimes, I think that "creativity" is equated with *stuff*. With having all kinds of supplies. Like colourful pens, sticky notes of every hue and shape, markers, a ruler on hand, and on and on. But, first, you could have nothing more than your body and breath, and go deep into creative contemplation. Second, that's just not most people's lives—to have copious stuff of the 'right' kind, on the ready. We can use whatever you have; it's not the gear or the tools that make us creative.

To that end, I also wonder if we just consider creativity as coming from the mind. Like it's a thinking-through exercise only. Like we have to think "harder" to be creative. Yet I'm always wondering about the body. About where the body is in what we're doing.

I'm not suggesting that one does interpretive dance to an essay brainstorm (although you absolutely could, at the very least to get the ideas going). What I am suggesting is that body is often, if not usually, left out of most things to do with school. And creative thinking is no exception.

Our bodies can be wildly helpful in terms of getting our creative ideas going.

There are many ways you can support your learners here, especially if they're feeling "stuck" or like it's hard to get the creative juices flowing, asking them things like:

- What does "stuck" feel like in the body? Where is it located? What kinds of words come up around stuckness?
- When you scan that list of topics (for example), which one makes your heart leap a little?
- What does your gut or intuition suggest about how you'd like to do or begin that?
- When you have a "good idea," how do you *know* it's good? What feedback does your body give you?

Any kinds of questions you can pose to your learner about the somatic experience of creativity can help, especially if they're experiencing "writer's block," if they're "blanking out," if they say they have "no good ideas."

And using the body can also be helpful in terms of *preparing* ideation. Jumping, a quick walk, shaking, and maybe most fun of all, putting on 1 favourite song, a little loud even, and dancing one's heart out. No rules, no choreography, no audience, no judgment, getting not the creative juices but the literal breath and blood flowing.

Where ideas come from

To encourage more making, more ideating, more playing around with ideas, media, and formats, it can be fun to hash out with your kids, "where *do* ideas come from?"

You might share some of your best ideas, inspired moments, aha breakthroughs, and the innovative insights you've been most proud of or praised for.

You might also share, perhaps even more importantly and tenderly, the ideas that have flopped. The ideas you tried out but weren't met well. The ideas you initially thought were remarkable, but then turned out to be quite rubbish.

From what stuck to what slumped, sharing your creative peaks and valleys would be so captivating to your learner.

And, likewise, going into both *their* next-level, along with long-ago hare-brained, creative attempts would be great fun.

These would serve as terrific seed-planting for a conversation about where (good) ideas come from. Where were you, what were you doing, and how did it happen...when your most creative ideas emerged? And, for your learner, what were the precursors?

Rhythms and patterns to ideating can be creative themselves, and illuminating to your learner about setting oneself up for creativity. For example, is it something about the space that encourages new thoughts and new connections—switching up your contexts, sitting in a different spot, being in a new space, or seeing an old one from a new perspective.

Or, are there actual, direct brainstorming games you can suggest or play together? There's always "would you rather," but also word associations, imagining three random objects and how they might be used together, or plays on words, or co-creating stories.

There's straight-up time spent in nature, ideally moving. Without doing anything extra or intentional aside from the actual nature-walk or st/roll, time outdoors automatically encourages creative flow.

And, you can invite them to set up a solo or family "what if" wall, with sticky-notes available to write down any and all "what if" questions that pop up over a month or year. "What if we travelled around the world for a year?," "what if we all played hooky together as a family?," "what if we ate 1 apple and some broccoli every day for a year, would we feel any healthier?," "what if we got a second dog?," "what if...?," "what if...?," "what if...?"

It could be that you get your learner a journal or note-pad beside their bed so that they can jot ideas just before sleeping or just after waking. They might find that an open notebook invites more ideas to come.

It could be that they come to understand that through simple, "mindless" tasks, like folding and putting away laundry, ironing, or washing the dishes allow for new ideas and connections to come forward.

It could be that intentional, boundaried "creativity" time to doodle, fool around on a guitar, try lyric-writing for a song, goofing around with music samples, getting out the sewing machine and some scraps, heading out to the shed or garage and seeing what comes of leftover pieces of wood...that purpose-fully naming and setting aside time can be the thing that helps your learner enter into creativity and receive those sparks and flashes of inspiration.

It could be through independent, friend, or family excursions. To music concerts, to art galleries, to museums, to nature spots, to architecturally innovative buildings. Or, a bit further flung, on travels and adventures.

It could be through exploring beloved and new music. The way a song makes us feel, and letting the mind wander. Or, through time set aside to free-write, either to a prompt or as an open journal, letting the pen, and the spirit, go where it wants.

All to say, ideas come from many places. Yes, sometimes *as if* from nowhere. But seldom *actually* nowhere. So, what are those conditions? It's worth thinking, and talking, about with your learner.

165

Constraints: the most creative thing you can do

Anyone waiting for the muse to appear, to just knock at the door and announce, "I'm here, let's get creative," it's going to be a long wait.

Sometimes our learners—and us—fall into the trap of thinking that we can only be creative when we're "in the mood" or when creativity "strikes." But it's a myth.

To be sure, if we have hobbies or just like to dabble in an activity now and again, the "when I feel like it" approach can work great! But, in terms of school, if there's a project that requires creativity, *waiting* for a creative mood is simply another form of procrastination.

It's not that I don't believe we can't get inspired while we're just sitting there on the couch watching TV. This *can* happen.

But it's a risky thing to *plan* for.

If a learner has an assignment that centres on creative thinking or taking a creative approach—and I might argue, this is *every* project, whether creativity is asked for explicitly or not—waiting for the right mood or an available muse is precisely the opposite approach.

What might be painful for your learner to hear is that the most helpful thing you can do to nourish your creativity is to put it to use. And, to set constraints.

This may not land well, but it turns out that deadlines fuel creativity. Having to complete something, arrive somewhere, submit some kind of work by some date—fuels creation.

Having an open-ended, "whenever it happens" frame, which is no frame at all, promotes drifting, putting things off, and pushing work until another day.

Am I suggesting that your student has to go-go-go on their creative project around the clock? Never.

But, I do want to dispel a muse-waiting or muse-reliant stance.

Tim Pychyl, author of the remarkable book, "Solving the Procrastination Puzzle" illustrates a powerful point that I love to share with my students and clients. It's born from the world of athletes and training.

Does an athlete only train when they "feel like it?" No.

Do they wait for creativity to knock on the door, for that muse to just show up, or inspiration to "strike?" No.

There's something about this analogy that Pychyl makes that really drives it home. If we want something—or, if we *have to do* something—waiting for the energy to do it, or the mindset to do it, or the motivation to do it is a misuse of hope. It's too long a wait. It may never come to fruition.

Instead, by *doing* the thing—doing the project, or doing the training—*that* is what fuels that muse. It makes it likelier to *want* to do it the next day.

My dad used to say it like, "accomplishment begets accomplishment."

I might put it like, "when we do the thing today, it makes doing the thing tomorrow easier."

So the muse isn't random in her appearances. She shows up when we've started. When we're diligently practising and chipping away.

And, we begin to diligently practice and chip away when there *is* a clear frame or boundary—in the shape of a deadline. We have an end-date that we need to produce something for. We break it down, we commit a certain amount of time to devote to it each day or every other day, and we *don't* ask ourselves as the starting question, "do I feel like doing this today?," "am I in the mood?," "am I inspired?," "am I feeling *creative?*"

What's so beautiful is that we *will* feel like doing this today... once we're doing it, or once we've done it and are looking back.

We *will* be in the mood once we begin. We *might well* be inspired by our own diligence and commitment. We *nourish* creativity by starting and getting immersed in a project.

Waiting is seldom a fruitful strategy. Of course, we need patience to tend to an injury. We need time during grief. We need space after heartbreak, a big disappointment, or unsettling life changes.

I am not offering a blanket, "push through at all costs." But I am nudging for an "inspiration comes often *after* you start." And, that inspired, creative energy can come rushing in when we bring in time.

An end deadline. Milestones to get there. Micro-goals to get there. A time window *today* to put words to paper, strums to guitar, pencil lines to sketchbook.

Learners and professionals alike sometimes misunderstand the key ingredient to productivity. It's not wide-open space. It's clear boundaries.

Constraints energise what comes before. They make it clear that we don't have the rest of the day. That "getting to it *some*time" won't lead to much getting to it. Words written beget more writing more words; more painting begets more painting.

So, the next time your learner has a creative impulse but is waiting for that muse, encourage them to set constraints and get producing.

Get to know your wild side

Years ago, a colleague showed me a wonderfully, well, creative self-test on creativity. It's called "My Creativity Type" and is put out by the brilliant folks at Adobe Create. (I have no relationship with any of the folks who made and maintain this, nor do I benefit in any way from mentioning this site.)

It's free, it's fast, and it's so much fun. Wonderfully imaginative images, strange texture combinations, unexpected movement. It is the web-embodiment of creativity.

The point is *not* that everyone has or is a "type." You likely get the sense from my writing that I'm not at all into typifying.

I've never suggested this for a student, or done it alongside them, as way to *actually* identify a hard and fast creativity profile.

Instead, I use it as kindling for conversation and joyful reflection. You and your learner can try it out: https://mycreativetype. com/

The Adobe folks also make clear that they're not suggesting binaries or impositional ways of being. It's about our creative inclinations. It's about strengths and opportunities.

There's the Adventurer, full of buoyant energy for all kinds of things; there's the boundlessly innovative Visionary. And there are six other "types" that learners might find resonance with.

I think My Creative Types is about seeing ourselves generously. In this way, I think who might benefit most from doing this 'type-test' are learners who don't see themselves as "creative." Calling all parents of learners who *aren't* directly artistically inclined: let's pushback against "creative" being equated with the Arts exclusively.

Now, I'm a BIG fan of all things fine arts, culinary arts, dramatic arts, and movement arts especially. But I'm also a BIG fan of not believing that these are the only ways to be creative. All disciplines can be an art; daily life has all kinds of creative pockets. My Creativity Type is about ways of being—dispositions—not how creativity is enacted or practised. It gives language to the spirit we can bring behind whatever it is we're doing, whether it's gardening or coding or solving science problems or doing watercolours.

Raising creative learners

Creativity doesn't look like any singular thing. It's not one activity. It's not some people but not others. It's a kind of flow-through, an energy behind what we're doing, a mindset, an embodiment.

It can bring joy, and relief, to invite your kids into conversations about creativity—where it comes from, what its presence is in your life, what keeps you there, how you can channel it, and how to identify creative aspects of ourselves, even if we don't feel like they're easily discernible.

Where I see this conversation about creativity as being most helpful—whether in terms of talking with your learners about inspiration sources, constraints, or disposition—is when your learner *isn't* feeling all that creative. When they might feel stuck, in a state of stasis, or uncertain about their creativity.

It's there. We just need to coax or coach it.

Chapter Eleven

The Brilliance of Procrastination

Procrastination comes up—a *lot*—with my students, the parents I work with, and the professional teams I coach and train, and with almost every friend and colleague.

Getting stuff done, having too much to do, time pressures, feeling distracted, it's all in there. What to do first, next, and last, how long to do something for, where to start and how to know when to put work down. Procrastination envelops everything to do with time, work volume, interest and motivation, and focus.

When I'm asked about procrastination, it's always about how to stop procrastinating. How to put an end to it. How to catch it just as it's beginning to take hold. How to mitigate the fallout from it. How to not make it a habit. What *to do* about it.

What's never mentioned is how smart, how *brilliant* it is— what's underneath why students procrastinate.

How so?

Procrastination is perfectly adaptive; it reveals feedback as to missing skills, it protects learners from failure in the immediate, it leads to more fun and interesting things in the present, it frees us from challenging work, and it gives an instant reward.

Let's dive deep.

What's the feedback revealed in procrastinating? Firstly, there's an opportunity to strengthen time-management skills. There's a good chance that a learner who puts things off is having a tough time in their *relationship* to time. That's an opportunity for learning strategies. It reveals that along the way, perhaps they've not been taught the skills of planning and prioritising.

Good news! Time management learning strategies can be taught. And, there are so many things your student can learn and try.

What's the failure-protection element of procrastinating? If we don't do something, we can't fail at it. We can't embarrass ourselves, or let anyone down. Yes, we make the time tighter in which to accomplish the thing we need to do—and with each day that passes with procrastination, make failing more possible— but in the moment of avoidance, we don't have to deal with that. Or any of it. We shoved off those bad feelings, those fears, those "what if's," that tough inner critic, that relentless voice that might be saying, "you can't do it"—at least for a little while.

As to procrastination leading to engaging in things that are more presently compelling, that speaks for itself. If a learner finds an assignment boring, they might procrastinate to do something that's more interesting to them. And as we've explored about boredom being uncomfortable, it sure makes sense that anyone would want to avoid discomfort. It doesn't help with the underlying invitation to *be able* to sit with boredom, to tolerate discomfort; but it does add up that anyone would want to put the source off or push it away.

172

Certainly, procrastination gets a learner out of hard work. This is a high-consequence approach that only intensifies the thing being avoided—the hard work, of course, gets harder with less time to do it in and more stress surrounding it. But in the moment, in the evening of procrastination, the challenge goes away. If a learner is struggling with complex instructions, a multi-step assessment, a weighty writing piece that needs careful thinking through—these all go away, for a short while, with procrastination.

Finally, there's an instant reward: work goes away, pleasure takes its place, and your kiddo doesn't have to think about what they've been avoiding for a bit longer. Something easier, something more interesting, takes its place.

I'm going to offer procrastination prevention strategies below from a variety of different starting places. But it felt crucial—and humane—to enter into this chapter with an acknowledgement and normalisation of procrastination.

Comprehension

Even though it can be so hard for them to admit or say aloud, sometimes your learner might not understand the content or instructions. And can you imagine a better reason to procrastinate?

It can feel embarrassing, shameful, or even scary to admit to not really knowing what's going on. (It can be confusing, too, to even know or identify what we don't know.) Often, there are a barrage of parent responses when a kid says, "I don't know what this means," or "I don't know how to do this," or "I don't understand." Parents, often out of frustration and a natural inclination for worry and concern, might say sharply, "weren't you paying attention?," "how can you not get this? It's so easy...," "oh, come on, you're smarter than this."

Ouch.

So, one starting place for a learner who's procrastinating is a gentle check-in around understanding.

This isn't so easy. We don't want to, *ever*, imply our learner isn't capable, isn't bright, isn't thoughtful. So, finding out if it's a comprehension 'gap' that underlies procrastination, is delicate work. But it is possible.

You can have your learner read the instructions of the assignment they're avoiding aloud to you. If there's trouble with some words, that might be a flag. You can ask for clarification (even if you understand), "that's new to me, can you help me understand what that means?"

With gentleness and inquisitiveness, find a way to have your learner explain what they know about the assignment.

You can ask them what the hardest parts of the question or starting place is. This can help you clue in to whether your learner is struggling with the content or with the wording of a question.

You can ask, "what do you think your teacher is getting at?" or "what do you think is at the heart of this assignment?"

You can even ask, if you're finding it hard to get clear or if your learner seems a bit closed to talking about the work, "how would you design this assignment, or phrase this question, if you were the teacher?" This can make it feel a little safer to explore comprehension as your kiddo is now imaginatively role-playing the expert in the room.

These kinds of queries can help you see whether your learner grasps what the ask is, or whether they're missing the mark.

If your impression is that your learner is shaky in their understanding of the question or task:

- Identify and define any unclear wording; sometimes a quick dictionary look-up can do the trick.
- Support them in writing to their teacher or professor to ask for a check-in; help your learner craft the clarifying question(s) they might pose.
- Have your learner connect with a friend or peer from class to trade understandings, and approaches to starting.
- Encourage them to run the question through a free "translator" like Rewordify (I have no relationship with www. rewordify.com, nor do I benefit financially); this kind of digital resource helps simplify convoluted language.
- Ethical use of AI can help too, for example creating a prompt for a basic, unelaborated essay outline in order to get started on a complex assessment.

If your sense is that it's less about the specific phrasing or organisation of an assignment, and more about bolstering content comprehension:

- Delicately inquire if / when / at what point your learner experienced confidence in comprehension; was it from the first class, or did it drop off after an absence? See if you can help them identify a point in the course or semester and trace back what was happening. This can help them begin to mark a topic to start with in terms of skill-rebuild.
- Help your learner gather the already-offered resources; often, we jump to external videos, things to try, and tutors, all of which can be superb, but sometimes there's material to work with that the teacher has provided that's been forgotten. For example, has the teacher videoed lessons or lectures? Are there slide decks? Have extra practice

questions been provided? Are there links or databases in a textbook that can be explored? Nudge your learner to see what they have on hand yet might not realise.

- Encourage your learner to spend a little extra time with their teacher before or after class, or in office hours; the key is, especially if they feel intimidated or unsure of what to say or ask, helping them prepare a few questions they can ask. And, reassure your learner that it's okay for them to say to their teacher, "I'm not totally getting _____," or "could you please explain _____ to me again?"
- Scan what free stuff is online; now, this comes with a big caveat. This cannot take the place of your learner doing or trying to get actual work done. But after, or in a space in between, see if there's a video, a free online tutoring session, as long as it's resonant. Because we're in a time and context of quick fixes PLUS endless distractions, this rabbit hole comes with risks of further procrastination.
- Explore short-term tutoring or learning strategy coaching. A boundaried, back-on-track series of sessions with an educator who can help co-create a comprehension catch-up plan, like how to proceed with work while rebuilding understanding.

As parents, because it disrupts the hoped-for flow of a night or weekend, and in light of all we're trying to do in our professional and personal lives, hearing our kid say, "I don't get it," can feel agitating, and even outright angering, especially if we're just seeing the behaviour of procrastination and task-avoidance. But if our starting place is believing our learner, then we look to what that work put-off or push-off might be communicating about tenuous comprehension underneath.

Completion

Is it possible that your learner is procrastinating because there are prep parts they've not done?

For example, is there a book report or review due that they're avoiding...because they've not read or finished the book? Is there math studying towards a quiz or midterm that they're not doing...because they've not done the homework that leads up to the assessment?

It would be normal for a parent's response to be frustration and anger, but know that your learner doesn't want to be procrastinating. They don't want to have not read the book or be behind in their math homework. And know too that they're likely already internally punishing themselves.

I wonder sometimes about why our kids' lackluster energy around work can land as so aggravating for us. I know I've felt impatient or frustrated—I'm not proud of that, but I do want to be honest. It's so convenient and easy when our kids just "get it." When homework gets done, when they understand what to do, and when they do what they need to. It's harder for us when it's harder for them.

Why do you think that might be?

It could be our egos—about what happens when we project ourselves on our kids, and when they stumble or struggle. We wonder what we've done to make that happen.

But there's something else at play; just about everyone is moving at breakneck speed with so much on the go. When anything delays our plans, when something unexpected happens, or when there's a hiccup or hurdle, it can feel downright infuriating.

Underneath that, my guess is that we're all so super stressed that it doesn't take much more in terms of additional stressors to push us over the threshold of coping.

Then, when our kid is procrastinating, slow or avoidant in their work, not handing stuff in and we have to take time to talk with the teacher, sit side by side and explain the work, or research a tutor, our already crunched, constricted time becomes even more so.

So, in the situation of incomplete work, we get both stressed out of concern for our kiddo, and stressed for ourselves out of *more* to do, hold, and tend to.

What *can* we offer to our learner when it turns out that their procrastinating ways are really about the incomplete work required ahead of time?

- Help your learner make organised sense of what had been necessary (like crucial texts) and assemble the assessment question(s).
- Help them make a plan for how to "catch up" in non-shaming, little-by-little ways, like 5 pages at a time, 8 times in a day, scattered throughout the day for 5 days in a row in order to read a 200-page book.
- Help them use generative AI with integrity, asking for a brief synopsis and key quotes *along* with re-reading in order to stay grounded in what's happening and motivated by a helping hand.
- Help them become extra-efficient with their assessment by encouraging your learner to have the core question or assignment task visible and in front of them at all times; this helps with your learner catching up *to a purpose*, for

example to respond to a question, to answer a problem, or to write a critical review.

Sometimes learners can feel easily overwhelmed by "falling behind" and then feeling like they have to choose between keeping up or looping back. My preference is a humane schedule in which both co-exist. This would look like two clear windows of time, like an hour in the earlier part of the day, split into to half-hour blocks; and, an hour in the evening, also divided in half. In the initial two half-hours, the learner could rebuild what was missed; in the later blocks, keeping current.

The risk of going back to the start and only working linearly is that then your learner is out of sync for longer. But with careful planning—really getting that agenda out, calendaring the days, thinking through what can go where—your learner can stay present and get caught up.

From there, watch their willingness and capacity to do the asked-for tasks more promptly. If they're up-to-date with what they needed to prep or practice ahead of time, there's less of a lag to getting started on the bigger assessment work.

Confidence

Another aspect of procrastination is feeling down on oneself. Learners who feel like they're not good enough, like they're not enough, period.

If you feel like you don't or can't have a voice in class, or like you can't write or solve or perform as well as others, then it's easy to get discouraged. And *that's* a recipe for procrastination.

Shaky confidence—or *shaken* confidence from a past hurt or tough feedback—can be a reason some learners procrastinate

179

and put off what registers as adding to self-doubt, wobbly self-worth, or punctured self-esteem.

But, you can see what happens next. A tough blow that ends in procrastination only secures another tough blow—marks deducted for lateness, poor quality of work due to rushedness.

So, another starting point can be rebuilding that threatened confidence. How we feel about ourselves impacts our willingness to risk, to share our views, to commit to a piece of writing or creativity. It changes how intensely we might work on a physics, engineering, or math problem set. It can manifest as an inner critic that holds us back from posing questions, from following our curiosity.

The task then becomes *less* so the work one and more so a learner's inner sense of (strong) self.

How to do that?

- First, building up the skill itself. As an example, if your child bombed a math quiz or chemistry test, the first route to confidence-cultivation is through more practice. Start studying more days in advance of the timed assessment, practise in shorter bursts, and zero in on the material that feels less certain (than what your learner consistently gets correct when practising). It's not that practice makes perfect, it's that practice makes confidence.
- Second, get granular with goals to make it more accessible to experience wins; a sense of accomplishment can go a long way, and micro-aims achieved, one after another, can nourish confidence and a self-belief of "I *can* do this."
- Third, seek out feedback, but initially from affirming sources. I'm *not* suggesting seeking out feedback that is exclusively affirming. What I *am* suggesting is to look for

critical feedback but from affirming people. There are some—maybe even many—who by lack of awareness, prior hurts, disconnection, can't hear how they come across, or who believe that tough words will lead to soaring success. I see it go the other way. So, if your learner is actively (re)building their confidence, yes to having them get responses to their work, including questions and challenges and suggestions, but no to laying bare a tender heart in front of a teacher or family member who lists towards rudeness.

- Fourth, help your learner remember all their extraordinary ways of being, things they've created, values they embody, high roads they've taken, important issues they've stood up for. They can picture it like stacking blocks or laying bricks; have them name as many wins and triumphs as they can. It might feel awkward, but it can be clarifying, if not inarguable, to see one's accomplishments itemised. They can feel especially absent if we're focused on what we've not done, or not done well enough.

It could be that the biggest takeaway for you here, and for your learner in tending to their confidence in these ways is that it is a skill and a practice. When confidence is running low, you and they can take comfort that it can be refuelled.

It's not so much that some folks are born with confidence and stay that way. Life's knocks, unexpected twists, hurts encountered, and things that didn't go our way, can all make us feel wobbly in our confidence. And, from there, pushing new, challenging, even exciting schoolwork away to stay in a safer, albeit it ultimately risky, place.

If your learner is procrastinating, consider confidence as the route to them getting more work done on time.

Compassion

Teach your learner the importance of, and practices to enact, self-compassion.

Of all the reasons that learners procrastinate, perfectionism is a big one. It is truly a doozy. It can be so pervasive for some learners, and so punishing.

I've had learners not hand work in that was done, ready, and in their backpacks.

I've had learners not start a major paper until hours before it was due, despite months of lead time, out of gripping fear that it wouldn't be good enough.

I've had learners stew for hours over the opening line of an assignment.

Perfectionism can get learners in its grip and be very difficult to shake off. It's critical for me to mention: if your learner is so caught in perfectionism that they are losing sleep, that they are repeatedly not handing work in, then please check in with a trusted mental health professional. Perfectionism is closely linked with anxiety and can be one of a number of "symptoms" around fear and control. So, if your observations are that your learner is experiencing perfectionism on overdrive, where it is impacting health, sleep, well-being, and academic performance, seek a supportive ally who can provide care and interventions.

If your learner seems to you to be more mildly perfectionistic—present but not persistent seeking of reassurance, dismissing excellent work as not good enough, or feeling disappointed in an A (instead of an A+) then consider giving compassion-based learning strategies a try.

- Translate your inner angry critic into the gentle voice of grandparent.
- Insist on treating yourself as you would a beloved friend.
- Actively reminding yourself that *everyone* makes mistakes.
- Disrupt the word "perfect" and get clear on how *nothing* actually is.

For perfectionists, creating spaces and experiences of comfort can be of help. If your learner is always clenched, always tight in their muscles, then practicing restorative yoga poses like putting legs up the wall or even lying on the floor, knees bent, feet flat on the ground—can creative physical ease to, over consistent repetition, support mental ease.

Additional strategies that can be of support:

- Check-in with your learner about expectations; what are they aiming for, what do they believe is possible or necessary, and what do they imagine will happen if they *don't* get perfect?
- Invite them to ask themselves the *lifelong* question, "how can I take care of myself right now? What do I need to feel grounded, clear, and well?"
- Limit social media scrolling: doctored photos, snippets of glamorous stories, and successes shared that leave out all of the hurdles and failures along the way. These things can add to the burden a perfectionist-tending student feels; protect them from this, or help them clearly see the harm of these images and stories, encouraging them to protect themselves from engaging.

Raising planful learners

Procrastination has us up all night, has our backs against the wall, has us panicked at times, has us uncomfortable and rushed. But it also protects us. It's a very clever form of adapting—to the tasks, projects, and to-dos that scare, ruffle, or unsettle us. Instead of us lamenting as parents, judging or criticising our learners' tendency to put things off until the last moment, or beyond, there is an underlying wisdom to procrastination.

Procrastination not only gets a bad rap, which makes sense as it leads to more stress and suffering, but it also comes with considerable shaming. Yet, we all do it.

Procrastination is brilliant in the simplest way, in the most immediate. It gets us what we need, and out of what we don't want to do.

It's just that, left without learning strategies like those explored here, procrastination ultimately winds up with making all that went *into* why a learner was procrastinating—worry, boredom, fear—*worse*.

Chapter Twelve

An A+ in Wayfinding

Many parents might say that the ultimate goal for our learners is to "do well" at school. But what does "doing well" mean? What does it comprise—what is "doing well" *made* of?

Some might say it's a journey to learn how to get good marks. That a learner is "doing well" if they're getting A+'s, if they're consistently performing at a "high" level, if they're "top" of their class.

Some might say it's about a way of behaving in class. Are they in a good and respectful relationship with their teacher, are they responsible, are they trustworthy—or are you getting calls home and dealing with situations to triage?

Some might say it's about making one's way through the social pieces. To find and nurture healthy friendships.

All of these might be right. But I'm driven to reveal the *how* underneath the hovering assumptions in "doing well."

If we take "doing well" to mean achieving strong grades, I want to uncover the "how" of those good marks. The strategies of listening, focusing, reading, writing, collaborating, studying, test-taking, and presenting that *lead* to strong grades—grades are in many ways just the outcome of a process. And, more deeply than that, to explore the awakeness and awareness and choice-points underneath that very listening, focusing, and so on.

Likewise, if we take behaviour and *behaving* well to be at the heart of *"doing* well" then I want talk about what hidden expectations there around what politeness looks like, what's meant by "respect," how to navigate power-filled relationships like teacher-student, bias, and forth—how relationships are *performed*. Similarly, how to *do* relationship, reciprocity, and mutuality.

Even with learning strategies that aim to do this work of revealing the how, "doing well" is also in part understanding the systems that underlie the school journey. And I'm not sure that this is spoken of so often.

There are some students who, because of their parents' advocacy, skillfully move through the labyrinth of school. There are many other students, more by far, who don't have this insider awareness; whose parents aren't privy to the inner-workings, don't have the access or the language, or know the workarounds and next steps when confronted by hurdles.

We'll explore how the things underneath the ways school happens are also part of a learner's "doing well." A big part. Whether we like it or not. Whether we understand it or not. Whether we agree or not.

K-12 wayfinding as parent advocacy

In the earliest years, we parents are the driving force behind getting our learners the help they might need.

By no means am I saying that we're in it alone. There are many educators in a school ecosystem that notice our kids' stumbles, imbalances, tendencies, and opportunities for support. It doesn't always happen. It's by far from smooth. But the school environment can have lots of helpers who pay attention to our kids along the way.

But, after noticing, then comes action-taking. And this often comes with a lot of late-night research, calls and visits to specialists, second and third (and fourth) opinions. We want to get it right for the people we love the most. Especially when we're worried about them.

Perhaps something isn't feeling quite right about how their learning is going. Or, something about your learner's mental health feels like it needs attending. Lots can get our spidey-senses tingling, and from there, as parents, we deep dive.

We do the lion's share in the first legs of the elementary to high school learning marathon. Over time, that advocacy begins to get shared, and then eventually shifts over to your learner. Our part wanes to some extent.

But if you've never done it, advocacy might not feel so straight-forward. How do you start? How do you know *what* to advocate for on behalf of your child? And when do you pass the baton to your developing child?

The first step of advocating on behalf of your child is your intuition. You could argue, perhaps, the place just *prior* to advocating, but it feels worth mentioning here. If you suspect that something's not quite right. If you sense that your learner is struggling with something and is having a hard time naming it, articulating what's going on, coping with it, or cultivating or implementing strategies, then follow that hunch. No one knows your learner better than you, particularly in the earlier years. Your child will eventually become their own best expert, but for some time, they need you to lean into your gut.

Tied for first step is also to talk with your kid. To listen. To believe them. If they say that something isn't going quite right in their understanding, capacity to concentrate, or do the work, hear them out. Sometimes, we just jump to "laziness," or to a diagnosis of some kind. But there's a lot of grey area. Hear your learner out, always.

Next is relationship. Right from the start of the year, build healthy, respectful, boundaried relationships with your kiddos' teachers. *If* you can, attend curriculum nights, parent-teacher conferences, and parent and school council nights. I know that what I'm saying will be a luxury for some. Many parents simply won't have the time or capacity. I'm just encouraging you to participate *if* you can make it work. These are one-off meetings and can go a long way to building trust and communication pathways from teacher to parent. They're definitely not the only way, so please don't feel badly or guilty or worried if you can't.

I also think that while participation is key to relationship, so is kindness. As a long-time educator, I've been on the receiving end of brusque parent emails. Ones that would be sent outside of business hours and demanding a quick response turnaround. Ones that were many paragraphs long. I *know* in my bones the fear and worry that underlie this kind of communication.

And, I know the impotence or resignation a teacher can feel when they're trying *so* hard all day long with several dozen learners, all with distinct needs, keeping things creative and attuned, only to be met by a challenging email from a parent.

I also live as a parent, experiencing the frustration of lacklustre pedagogy, approaches to teaching or assessment that have me in full head-tilt bewilderment, and unanswered (kind) emails to serious concerns.

My starting place, as parent, as educator, is one of benefit of the doubt. Of that most gracious and spacious interpretation. Parents are worried, teachers are stressed. Parents are on high alert, teachers are spread so very thin. Parents are overworked, teachers are overworked. Parents and teachers are humans trying their very best.

So, relationships that can get underneath all this, can be humane and helpful. I'm *not* suggesting building parent-teacher relationships as a "strategy," but I am suggesting that relationship is central to everything. Knowing your kids' teachers, them knowing you, having an easeful path of communication, know-ing their priorities as an educator, them understanding your family context and pressures, are all helpful.

In addition to intuition and relationship, proactivity is crucial. If you feel like something is "up" with your learner, you don't have to wait, hope that it will sort itself out. With care and respect, bringing wonderings, mis-givings, uncertainties to your learner's teacher is encouraged!

At that same time, joining your school's social media page(s) if they have, and your local neighbourhood ones, can help by providing space to pose wonderings. "I'm noticing that my kid is doing this, anyone else experience that...?" can be a helpful sharing. It's not about web-searching or crowdsourcing diag-noses, but rather community-building around a common won-dering or concern and shame-busting through heartfelt sharing.

These are all the supportive, surrounding pieces. Along with these, what can you do as a parent-advocate?

Jot down what you're seeing with your learner. Is it about a relentless spacing out, gnawing worry, isolation or withdrawn-ness, letters or numbers being written in disorienting or unclear ways, eyes jumping all over the place when reading, no reading happening at all. Try to name what it is you feel is going on for your kiddo. It's okay if it's a cluster, and if it's confusing. You're not a diagnostician, nor is your teacher, and you don't have to be. It's about a sharing and a trading of what you see at home and what your teacher sees during the day.

Then, form your question(s). It's likewise okay if you're not totally sure what to ask. Like we say to our learners, "just do the best you can." Having even half-formed questions helps you remember what's at the heart of your conversation with the teacher, and know if it was a fruitful conversation—if the wondering you went in with was attended to in some way.

Request a meeting with your child's teacher. It can be in-person, video-chat, or by phone. And it may be that one meeting won't be enough. But it's a start.

What kinds of things can you advocate for?

- You can ask your learner's teacher to keep an intentional eye out for your kid.
- You can ask for flexibility on a specific assignment.
- You can ask for a bit more choice or mode of expression for an assessment.
- You can ask for an occasional, regular check-in to see if there are changes for your learner.
- You can ask for an IEP—an individualised education plan—which outlines helpful accommodations for a learner, like extra time on tests.
- You can ask for additional in-school supports, like a school psychologist.
- You can ask for suggestions, from the teacher and school administration, for in-community resources, for example an OT or speech therapist referral.

You can see the arc here:

- Trust your gut; you know your kid.
- Believe your kid.
- Get to know your kid's teacher.
- Prioritise good, kind relationships.
- Make note of your concerns.
- Identify questions.
- Have (a) conversation(s) with your learner's teacher.
- Advocate for what you feel your learner might need.

In the earliest years, you'll be writing these emails, you'll be having these meetings. But as soon as you feel it's appropriate, include your learner. They'll be able to best speak to their experience. And, they'll experience modelling advocacy—they'll be holding the reins soon enough.

With their presence, you'll be able to get it more right—what it is that's happening for them. They can clarify or correct. And being able to identify and speak about what one needs is really at the heart of things.

From parent- to self-advocacy

In some ways, much of what it means to advocate on behalf of your child holds for when your learner is not their own primary advocate: intuition, deep knowing of oneself, relationship, kindness and care, noticing, ask questions, suggest and try things out, keep checking in.

But now, your learners are driving this bus.

They will need to, for example, craft those thoughtful emails. Teach them how! I do this with my post-secondary students ALL the time, right from the clear subject line that helps the reader triage its importance, to getting the spelling of their addressee's name right, to the kind hello, to the clear ask, to the warm sign-off, to when it's appropriate to send.

But what does it really mean *to* self-advocate? It's phrasing that gets used often yet is seldom made transparent. Given that it matters so much, *how* do learners do it?

Self advocacy is the ability for someone to effectively communicate their own needs, rights, and interests. It is a speaking-up on one's own behalf.

The thing is, it gets even more nuanced. Self-advocacy is also about making informed decisions. So, you can see where the learning strategies element fits in. It's about how we listen with as much single-mindedness as we can muster. It's about how we pay attention as closely as we can. It's about asking questions, how we take notes so as not to forget anything, and it's about what we do with those notes after any meeting or discussion.

How do we do these things?

To listen with single-mindedness, we can:

- Ensure we hear the person speak, and ask them so to speak up or slow down if we're finding things unclear or dizzying.
- Keep our gaze on them as often as we can; not in an awkward or alienating way, just instead of looking at our paper, our phone, or around the space.
- Watch the activities we engage in prior, for example if we can put off a conversation with a friend or family member that has a high likelihood of intense emotions until *after* a meeting that'll require skillful listening and self-advocacy.

To pay close attention, we can:

- Reduce external distractions, like putting a phone away.
- Plan any meeting in which self-advocacy skills will be called upon at a time of day when we're likelier to be more alert.
- Move, get exposure to light, eat well, and hydrate before a meeting so that we've nourished our capacity for concentration at the outset.

To ask good questions, we can:

- Jot a few down ahead of time, or even key topics or words to jog our memory, making it easier to pose those critical questions during a meeting.
- Ask clarifying questions throughout to ensure understanding, like saying, "can I repeat this back to you to make sure I'm understanding?"
- Release some pressure by reassuring ourselves that we might not get all our questions right, and that we can always loop back via email after with additional questions.

To take supportive notes, we can:

- Come with our supplies ready and considered ahead of time, for example a notebook, a pad and paper, a binder that has pockets for forms or additional sheets of paper.
- Ask for AI note-taking support during an online meeting so that we can fully focus and allow auto-transcription to take care of the written pieces.

- Let go of the fear that we must write down *everything* and instead lean into our listening and attention and jot down essential words, next steps, and additional questions.
- When we break all of this down, there's *a lot* to it!

There's also crucial work prior to any meeting that invites or invokes self-advocacy. For instance, to effectively communicate the needs you have means to understand them. *Feel* them. To be able to put them into words that can land clearly enough to be understood. And none of this is easy! It requires time for reflection. Time for self-inquiry and understanding. So many of us are busy in our days, sometimes not able to feel what it is that we need. Not to mention, sometimes we're reared to think we have to accept the contexts or systems we're in, even if they're harmful, so we might not even feel *allowed* to sense our needs, or to have any at all.

Then, after identifying them, to *speak up* for oneself about needs, is essential but not everyone feels they can. Not everyone is included or allowed to do this. Many are silenced or ignored. Many are put off or pushed to the margins. There's nothing easy or universal about self-advocacy. It's complex and layered.

But by airing out these pieces, by giving waypoints into how to do the elements of self-advocacy, we can practise, little by little, taking up space, using our voice, feeling into and expressing our needs, and making requests.

Making the most of the journey

Aside from advocating on behalf of your learner, or fostering in them the skills they need or will need to advocate on their own behalf, these are just part of "what *really* goes into doing well" at school. There are some wonderful opportunities that if parents don't know, or if parents didn't experience themselves, can pass a learner by. I want to pull back that curtain and share a bunch with you here!

As the years of a learner's schooling journey pass, the opportunities multiply.

In K–12, you can keep your ears and eyes open for:

- In-school mental health, social emotional learning, and OT support, right there in your learner's day. It won't be everywhere, but it will be in many places. And I'm not talking about in private or independent schools, I mean in many public education institutions, there can be more in-house supports than we realise. It just might not be visible. For example, there can be school psychologists that visit four schools in a district such that your learner doesn't naturally encounter them, but by connecting with the teacher or principal, you never know what you'll uncover.
- There are all kinds of free school-adjacent skill-building programs that you can sleuth out. Things like language and heritage activities, before / during / after school free / low-cost / subsidised STE(A)M programming.

As for post-secondary, the free offerings grow exponentially. For newly accepted students:

- There might be meet n' greets with other incoming students, often as early as the spring prior to the fall's start. Encourage your learner to go. It helps them get a feel for the place, for the staff, and have friendly faces when the semester starts.

- In the summer prior to the academic year, your learner can take a look for *pre*-orientation supports, particularly around learning skill-building. These have long since been around—not universally, but frequently—and have become more since the pandemic to meet concerns around students' *unreadiness* for the math, science, and writing demands of university or college courses. These often come with "boost" language, aiming to bolster academic skills.
- Orientation week is just about everywhere, and students have certain expectations or looking-forward-tos about this week, but encourage your learner to check their institution for any *alternative* orientation offerings. The big crows, the rah-rah-rah, these can be a lot for many students. There are very frequently alternatives, either built into these welcoming weeks, or adjacent to them. If your learner is a full "no" to orientation, help them scour the itinerary for one-off activities they might enjoy. Staff who plan these weeks are increasingly aware that the big parties are not for everyone.
- "Weeks of Welcome" are another thing to take a look at. Generally lasting the first six weeks, there are orientation-like activities that keep new students gathering for the first half of the semester. Why? This is a challenging transition time and post-secondaries are keen to *keep* their new students.
- Go on a campus tour! In-person and virtual tours happen regularly and help begin that connection-building.

For settled in new students and all other years:

- Workshops. You will never see more workshops *anywhere* than at a higher education institution. From academic citations to moving through intense shyness, how to make the most of LinkedIn for student employment to crafting a thesis statement.

- Supplemental Instruction. This phrase is one of the instigators for this chapter. There are *so* many things that students can participate in that they are often unaware of—*because* of how many things students can participate in. And parents are then even less in the know about what's possible. Supplemental Instruction, sometimes called other things, is facilitated group learning support. It's offered for classes that are commonly failed by strong upper year students; the aim to re-walk students through the challenging concepts encountered in class. It's like a failure-prevention initiative.
- Free tutoring. There are 1:1s that your learner can book with math, writing, and more. Your learner can even, for example, book a writing consultant session not having even started a paper but with the assignment sheet in hand go over *how* to start or craft an outline.
- Advising. This is such an underrated support. There are teams of advising professionals on every campus that literally explain how to navigate their courses and programs. They talk about prerequisite courses, what happens if you fail, how your learner is progressing through their degree. The job title, "Advisor" doesn't quite reveal the full beauty of this role; it's about how to get through on a very technical level. There's also motivational support offered, encouragement, and lots of connection with other campus resources. But from the start of your learner's degree, please get them to go to an advisor, build a friendly relationship, and begin to map out a plan. And,

certainly if your learner is stumbling along the way, or is considering dropping a course, an advising session will make a world of difference.

There are tailored supports, resources, and communities for your learner to know about:

- Cultural affinity. Black Excellence and mentorship opportunities, Indigenous student communities and programs, South Asian student groups; how you identify will very likely be met at a post-secondary. If this is important to you then I hope it was part of your search criteria when you applied and accepted.
- English-language support. From conversation circles to meet-ups, if your learner has English as an additional language, there are many ways to both practice *and* connect with other students.
- Religious, linguistic, athletic, values-based groups abound. It's worth an exploration.

Accessibility in post-secondary. Ultimately, you and your learner need to know that there is a disability services office—sometimes with the words access or accommodation used instead—on every campus. Each will have similar but specific intake processes. Documentation requirements, like medical information, will differ from site to site. And, the scope of offerings will be unique as well: some will have in-house psychoeducational assessment opportunities, an on-site assistive / adaptive technologist, an on-staff occupational therapist. If your learner has a disability, whether physical, sensory, learning, or psychological, it is worth connecting with that disability services office as early as possible *prior* to the start of their first year. These offices are available anytime—new diagnoses, injuries, flares, illnesses, and updating documentation—but if you *know* that you will require accessibility-related accommodations, then a check-in about process and docs is highly recommended.

More on accommodations. There are two pieces I want to share as someone who has worked in higher education for 15 years.

First, your learner doesn't have to register with this office. There is no obligation. Many students choose to navigate their academic journeys by individually asking each teacher for the accommodations they need—extra time on tests, extensions on assignments. These offices are there for students who wish or require *facilitated* accommodations, meaning that there is set process to follow—a letter that gets sent to a learner's profs outlining the accommodations to be honoured. Second, accommodations can also come from a few places. May there never be a need, but if your learner seeks support from a gender-based violence office on-campus, they can put in place things like extensions; so can mental health offices. These aren't often made transparent, so I'm keen to share that here. If your learner experiences a traumatic incident, there are behind-the-scenes channels to help preserve their academic journey, and you and they should know that.

Sometimes, big things happen that make it feel impossible to do school, but "dropping out" is only one possibility. This is the other really important thing to share with you and your student. As an adult, you *know*. You have lived that anything can happen. The big hurts, losses, accidents. When these happen for students, it can make going to class or handing work in untenable. That's why you and they need to know about "incompletes" or "petitions." This is where a three month or semester long extended window is created for your learner in which to accomplish the work. It requires a little bit of paperwork—usually not much. Your learner would get in touch with their instructor and potentially their advisor and be let through the straightforward process.

Other things that aren't usually shared openly:

There are make-up tests and exams if your learner is sick or in a flare.

- If your learner disagrees with a grade, they can "petition" it and ask for reconsideration.
- Grade or full-year "forgiveness" options, where students going through tough times can re-do a course and have the second grade be the one that counts, or have a year's worth of class marks waived and do it again.

Student employment. This is its own field, so while the offerings are robust, I'll aim to keep it brief:

- As your learner is applying, have co-op as a criteria to consider. It's not available in every program, and it's not for everyone—time and cost. But, know that work placements *as part* of the learning journey are on offer.
- Career centres. Your learner's institution will have a built-in career hub where they can get support in finding an on-campus student staff job, in-community employment, and all the steps along the way, from cover letter help to practice interviewing.
- Experiential education. This is increasingly enfolded into the academic journey. It means, in addition to co-op, things like placements in a course, what's called "Work-

Integrated-Learning" (WIL), guest lectures in classes *about* employment connections, business-based mentorship. It's worth checking out.

This is far from exhaustive. There are literally a whole book's worth of additional offerings and insider tips, so your best bet is to spend concerted time with your learner—or have them do it and tell you about what they find—exploring their campus' website. Not everything will be there, but much will be. It's particularly important in terms of process (like international students and visas), community (what student groups are available), campus events (to build that connection), and *people* (helpers in your learner's faculty, and across the institution) who can help guide, swoop in, intervene, and support.

Raising informed learners

Why is all this worth including as a chapter in this book? Because these are equally important pieces to keeping your learner well *in* learning spaces. Because the offerings and processes are often *so* opaque. "How does anyone find out about this stuff?" is something I hear from parents. Because I've been on the inside for years, encountering learners who don't know or make use of even a fraction of what's offered until the very end, until a friend mentions something, until a poster catches their eye—and invariably, "I wish I'd known about this sooner!" Getting top marks in mathematical problem-solving, in science experiment write-ups, in essay-crafting, or on multiple choice tests in the humanities, these might all be worthwhile goals. And, to be sure, they can support what comes next—more schooling, internships, apprenticeships, work experience. But, even more useful than picking-up content is to learn the skills of navigating systems. We can help our students in clear, direct ways to get what they need—to find the at-school resources, off-campus supports, the in-community go-tos that are seldom-to-never spoken about transparently.

Chapter Thirteen

Belonging and the Wild Card of Connection

Another school secret rarely shared with parents, or students, is the central place of "belonging" to academic success.

It's a magic potion that's not revealed.

Ask any student, "what's the key to your success at school?" What are they likely to say?

"Paying attention in class," "getting work in on time," "doing well on tests," or even more generically (and a little defeatedly), "doing what my teacher says."

What are parents likely to respond with?

"Trying hard." "Studying hard." Generic, common, generationally passed down phrases (we all inherited them).

Bringing them together, a collective idea is that students "do well" when they do what they're told, and bring effort to it.

But the secret revealed is that the primary factor that accounts for a student staying—"persisting" as it's sometimes called—is belonging. *Feeling* and *knowing* that they belong.

"Belonging" is its own field of study, particularly in teaching and learning, and education writ large.

Virtually no student or parent has had this shared with them, and yet it's the most vital element to doing well. We can't get to where we want to go without a sense of community, affinity, and welcome. When doors and windows and pathways are closed, where there is harshness and exclusion, where there is one "no" after another, where there is nothing that lets us know we're safe and invited and can use our voice and can take up space, these make it infinitely more challenging to participate, engage, and keep going. If we are messaged to and told that we don't belong, whether directly or in every other way, it makes showing up and staying *very* difficult.

Back to school and performance. More often than not, it *looks* like great grades are the result of "doing as told" and "trying hard," along with other common assumptions like talent, parental involvement or encouragement, extra help like piled-on tutors, or a lucky encounter with an inspired teacher. That a student who excels at school is all about how much they're willing to give of themselves, the ultimate being the all-nighter.

It's not.

The number one variable that accounts for student success, more than any other, is *belonging*.

In other words, nourishing some kind of enduring connection with a teacher, staff member, professional, or supportive peer network at a school.

Why?

Belonging is what helps learners feel safe and in-the-right-place when sitting in a classroom or lecture hall. It's what en-ables a student to say "hello," or maybe even more than a quick greeting, to their course or program peers. It's what encourages a student to sign up for an intramural team, join the recreation centre for the first time, head to a student group meet-up, or go to a school sponsored event. To belong is to be linked to, have a right place in, or have a home in. Belonging is also where referrals, mentorship, and potential future work are born.

At the core of belonging is *relationship*. And I see it as an ecosystem, or like concentric circles expanding outward.

As a learning strategist, I'm always thinking about the *how*. So, how *do* learners *do* belonging? How does belonging get practised?

Relationships. It's *always* relationships.

Relationships with teachers and instructors is paramount. Having these be positive and trusting, consistent and non-shaming, representative and welcoming. It's less important that prof be funny, gregarious, entertaining, and larger-than-life to their students—sure this is fun, but it's not crucial. What's more important is for a teacher to ensure that their students—and *any* student they encounter—feels like they belong. *Knows* they belong. In the fullness of their identities and worries and stresses and challenges. Whether an A+ student or a learner who is struggling with failing marks. Whether a student with flawless attendance, or one who has a tough time making it to class on the regular. Each and every student belongs, and instructors need to ensure this is felt and known.

Through relationship, we find trusted allies to help through the stumbles and setbacks—staff encountered along the way, class colleagues. But, the belonging circle broadens to also include the physical campus and building a connection with the actual spaces, as well as seeking out opportunities for global belonging through international opportunities.

This chapter shares all of these and more—and, emphasised most of all, are ways that parents and chosen families can support students' in finding their people and places, and why these belonging-based relationships enhance, rather than detract from the learning journey.

Belonging by way of teachers and instructors

Belongingness can start by building a relationship with a teacher—safe, ethical, boundaried. Sometimes, students see their teachers as content purveyors, graders, and intimidating gatekeepers. (And, sadly, it can feel like that in some instances.)

But, it can also be that a teacher is the key to a student's sense of welcome. To them feeling like they belong.

In the early, middle, and high school years, teachers can make or break the learning experience for students. Not just academically. But also in creating and ensuring for each learner that the classroom and school, and learning more broadly, are safe places where the learner is welcome in full, exactly as they are. This is such an important time period in terms of identity formation, self-belief, creative expression, community-building, and amassing healthy coping and resiliency skills. The teacher is crucial in these.

How can parents help?

Back to building relationships with teachers, encouraging learners' self-advocacy, as we've explored, as well as bringing new ideas and education trends to principals. While writing this book, I met an amazing learning scientist—bold, skillful, brilliant. A mom of three, she was in conversation with her eldest kiddo's school principal and they wound up talking teaching and learning. This being her passion, she shared her heartfelt insights about evidence-based teaching strategies that she's *not* seeing in schools. Wouldn't you know, the principal said, "I had no idea. That wasn't how I was taught, it's not how most teachers are educated. But that makes so much sense."

Most of all, I think there's something to be said about how families hold conversations about teachers. Is it pejorative or is it compassionate, is it being part of the complaint bandwagon or is it supporting a learner in finding their way into a dreaded assignment, is it hostile or is it encouraging of dialogue with the teacher? I think kids learn so much more than we realise from our modelling of how we hold their teachers in high regard, or not. Whether we're generous with our interpretations. It's not rose-coloured glasses, it's not avoidant of injustices. Instead, it's about instilling in our kids the worthwhileness of good relationships, where possible, with their teachers.

As learners continue their scholastic journey, teachers take on ever-changing roles in their lives. Where in earlier years, they *can* be trusted allies and offer guidance, while these can still happen in post-secondary, there's also the possibility of an educator being a professional mentor for a learner.

Through student staff, RA (Research Assistant), TA (Teaching Assistant), GA (Grad Assistant), and other formal work arrangements, mentorship can take place. But it can also be informal, emerging out of a keen student showing up for office hours, asking questions for additional readings or clarification, and taking an interest in what an instructor is researching and writing. Relationship in this sphere can become more curiosity based with shared interests. When your learner encounters a resonant instructor, urge your learner to purposefully connect with them, ask for 1:1 time, make use of class office hours, and apply for assistant roles.

Post-secondary educators can also become point people for skillful, warm referrals—to accessibility, mental health, and other key services on a campus. Encourage your learner, if they're feeling unsure about their program, if they're looking for more support, to ask their prof if that's become a trusting relationship.

Of course, there will be instructors who don't make space for this kind of connection. And that's okay too. You can let your learner know that there are all kinds of complex intricacies for instructors—some are low-paid, contracted educators, living from one precarious semester to the next, and may be doing that in three separate institutions, all while raising a family and trying to publish their work in hopes of more secure employment. I know educators in these positions—*many* folks like this—who are so tight on time that even crafting a reference letter is an "extra" they just don't have capacity for. Your role here is both as encourager, and as a humaniser—helping a learner understand why they might not be hearing back from their prof, why their favourite instructor just doesn't seem to have time for them.

But where there's an opening, whether in the early or later years, that teacher-student connection can be a life-changing one. When a learner stumbles into that educator who sees them, gets them, and even looks out for them, this is its own, profoundly meaningful kind of belonging.

Belonging by way of staff

There are so many staff members that a learner will encounter throughout their years. Front desk folks, advisors, consultants, counsellors. And these relationships can also be key to a learners' success.

208

Similar to instructors, when your learner feels that safe connection and resonance with a staff member, this can be such a win!

I've worked with folks for years who still get regular updates and visits from students who've graduated, not just for updates but for that touchpoint connection.

Sometimes, in the hierarchy of institutions, staff are seen as conduits. They facilitate connections, they "serve," they support. I'm not a fan of this thinking or language. Staff are who make things work. It's how it all happens. They're the financial support person who unlocks funding for a student and changes their life. They're the disability coach who provides a profound sense of relief for a student in understanding their first psycho-educational assessment. They're the intake support for the counselling office, the first person your learner sees in their initial, and may-be terrified, foray into psychological support.

Staff members are so important, and student relationships with these folks cannot be overstated.

As with every student-to-professional relationship, there needs to be clear edges and boundaries. And THIS is one of the MOST powerful conversations to have your learners. It's a discussion that, ideally, begins early in each household. What's mine / what's yours. What's okay / what's not okay. What's appropriate / what's a trespass. Consent. Respect.

What's a skillful question to ask here, but not there; when it's appropriate to write or visit, and when it isn't.

I've had students push up against my boundaries, feeling that warm care and affinity. But as professionals, there's nothing more essential than maintaining those boundaries. They're what keep both student and practitioner safe.

But the student has their part; which is to say, *you* have your part. It's such an essential one. You can have all kinds of lifelong conversations with your learners about those thresholds—how to feel and maintain them, and how to honour those of others.

Staff relationships are a great place to both build belonging, and to deepen conversations about safe, trusting, and boundaried relationships.

Belonging by way of peers

In the early years, parents' roles can be more active. You can invite your child's peers over and their parents to foster full-community, or encourage your learner to share in playdates and get-togethers with their classmates. These can be centered around games and fun, no mention of school. The influence of belonging doesn't have to be direct; it's around ensuring your learner experiences trust in the classroom, a web of connections.

In the middle years, belonging can be forged through school clubs and groups. These become more interest-based. It's not that your learner has to be involved in everything—I think we're all more aware of over-scheduling our kids and protecting time for them to decompress and recuperate. Learners can *start* a club if they have a passion for something that doesn't yet have a group. And, what's particularly wonderful about in-school activities is that there's usually a teacher connected to it. Sometimes, that teacher will be known to your child—perhaps a current or former instructor. Other times, it'll expose your learner to an entirely new educator, perhaps one they'd never have the chance to meet or learn from. These connection help widen the circle of care for your learner.

In the high school years, you can suggest to your child that they consider participating in things like student government or sports teams or performances. These comprise students from across the grades and interests, and there are different "roles" to play, from center-field or stage to supporting positions. In class provides opportunities for belonging as well, like purposefully starting conversations with peers that your child doesn't usually interact with—scary, yes, but doable over time. At first, a question. Then, maybe a genuine compliment. Maybe next, a small sharing of a weekend's happenings. Over time, a small relationship gets built. It doesn't have to become a best friendship. But, on-purpose relationship building is a skill, it can keep our kids connected, and it always leads to better engagement, and performance, in school.

In post-secondary, it's about nourishing a connecting to your learner's campus family. Their network to be. It begins with a warm hello when sitting beside someone in a lecture. From there, trading contact info. Then, and you can see the learning strategy woven in, having your learner suggest they trade notes in order to get insight about how another hears and jots things down. It also serves as back-up for your child if they're unwell, or to be in service of the other student if they're absent.

It's also about rallying or joining study groups, finding ways to establish relationships while immersed in the course. What I notice repeatedly is that a class is yearning for folks to gather energy. And this can feel so hard or awkward to do, but when someone happens to bring that spirit, that vibe, of rallying people it can come as such a relief. I've been in classes where no one does this; I've been in classes where on the first day someone says, "okay, I'm going to be that person, let's all just share contact info, I've made a WhatsApp group, let's do this!"

The latter is such a different experience. I've been absolutely awed, bowled over and wowed by that bravery. And, it changes the connection and cohesion, not to mention the helpfulness of being able to send a quick class text for clarification.

To *not* be strangers with the person beside you makes a huge change in what it feels like to be in class, and the motivation, participation, and engagement that ripples.

And, beyond the 1:1, sitting-beside relationships and the study groups, it can also be starting or participating in whole class WhatsApp groups. I've been part of these in grad school, and I've born witness to these as an instructor. They're SO helpful! Students can pose, shame-free, a question about an assignment date, for example—easier, perhaps, to post to peers when something is due than to ask the teacher (who'll remind that it's in their course outline, on the virtual course shell, in the five emails already sent, and written on the class whiteboard). Putting the query to class buddies carries virtually no chance of shame because they are likely wondering the same thing.

Study groups are also fantastic for building connection without the pressure of aimless conversation or uncomfortable get-to-know-yous. There's something already in common, and that's the premise for getting together. I can't tell you how many students I know who've made friends, and retained friends, from study groups along the way. Because, through relationship-building over course materials (and maybe bemoaning the teacher), little bits of personality and personal *life* sneaks in. People begin to share of themselves bit by bit.

The next way learners can access belonging via peers in higher ed is through student unions, program-related student organisations, hobby and interest-based groups. From playing quidditch to religious affiliation, the Psychology or Criminology or Midwifery Students' Association to the student union fighting for fairer tuition, there are so many ways learners can find friends, and purpose, and *belonging* at their school.

Belonging by way of the school

It can be the case that the architecture of the school buildings leave you and your learner cold. Other times, there can be a charm to the structures. Or, a beauty in the history. Some campuses have green-tech buildings, others have wildly artistic structures. Whether the physicality of the learning institution is leans towards the industrial or the avant garde, a learner can find their way to belonging to the spaces too.

Schools are fascinating places. I'm often left scratching my head at how ugly, uninspiring, or cold places of learning can feel. Other times, I'll see breathtakingly beautiful spaces that feel not just inspiring but *healthy*. That feel like a student can do school *and* be well. Natural light, access to fresh air, outdoor spaces. These are the dream, really. And I'm aware, and have lived (many times over), just how much this isn't the case.

And yet, a learner still goes, day in, day out. So, how can we encourage them to find and feel a sense of connection if not belonging to the built environment?

Two ways: study spaces and sit spots.

Study spaces can be a fun adventure to find. Students often stick to the school or campus areas they know. The places that are on their route. The hallways they walk every day. But, had their timetable been otherwise, they'd have had an opportunity to see different classrooms, lecture halls, corners, windows. It's just happenstance. So, strategy number one to nudge your learner towards, would be to sleuth out a place that feels conducive to quiet work.

In all levels of school, there can be small tables and chairs set up for silent work. There are libraries. On post-secondary campuses in particular, there are bookable spaces. There can be carrousels. There are lots of options, both formally intended for studying, and other lovely little corners that have no purpose but to gather.

Having your learner find *"their"* study spot can be a game-changer.

First, going to it and working can become as routine and set as going to a class. It's just a place that they go to at a recurring time. (And have your learner, if possible, seek this space out as early into a year or semester as they can *before* crunchy work times build so that there's an opportunity for continuity and for a habit to form.)

Second, it can become a place of community. Many students visit a place on the regular. It might well be that a new friendship sparks from seeing the same face week after week during this routine study time.

(Although this isn't formally about belonging, it means that studying is built in. It can really help a student get their studying done when they plan a weekly (or more frequent) time and spot to go to exclusively for this purpose.)

Third, is by finding a "sit spot." It's interesting to me that this notion of a sit spot is really alive in nature education, in early years learning, and in later-life retreats. Yet, it's seldom offered to adolescents and young adults.

A sit spot is a place of respite, ease, and connection.

That connection is the point.

Have your learner find theirs. It can be rooted in comfort—like a soft place to land in the midst of busy days. It can be rooted in aesthetic connection—like a student-run art gallery. It can be rooted in student culture—like that cool coffee club that's around the corner, down the hallway, and feels like a world away.

It's not the what, it's the *where*.

It can also be outdoors. Somewhere in a quadrangle; somewhere near a residence on the edge of a campus; a park bench two blocks from the school. But a favourite place to land.

A nook won't make or break your learner's experience, but it can be a sweet other way in to creating belonging.

Belonging by way of the physical environment

Learners at times, particularly when it feels drab or under-inspiring might consider school as an obligatory burden. It can be a struggle to get there on time, a struggle to rally and devote full attention, a struggle to identify the purpose or *want* underneath the, "I *have* to go to school."

Most literature on belonging focuses on the *people* of an institution. But I also want to honour the place itself.

Sometimes, relationships are just spoken of in terms of person-to-person, or pets, but what of our relationship to the natural world? I continue to learn so much from Indigenous elders and mentors, and the writers and thinkers who's work I immerse in. We are in direct relationship with the plant and animal life around us. So, to my heart and spirit, any conversation would be incomplete without mentioning the nature context in which a school or campus is situated.

To be sure, many will be tough and rough buildings in urban areas, seemingly devoid of natural life. I grew up in a downtown metropolis, so I get it.

But, that doesn't mean that there isn't birdsong, glimpses of a seasonal bird, or beautiful cloud formations and skies above.

I want to honour how much the physical environment matters to how we feel about a place.

Think about your home and the paint colours you've chosen, the furniture and fabrics, the lighting—these all impact how you feel. Even clothes—you likely have a favourite outfit. Why?

We are not immune to the energetic impact of where we're situated. I encourage learners to explore.

Belonging to the world

At risk of sounding too esoteric, I also wonder about a learner's experience of belonging to the *world*. Nearing the end of writing this book, one of my daughter's had just returned from a 5-day school trip to New York City as part of a Model United Nations delegate. It was life-changing.

Being *at* the UN headquarters, meeting children from around the world, walking the Brooklyn Bridge, and a quick visit to FAO Schwarz—she became transformed. More courageous, more self-assured. She'd practised navigating a new city, took all kinds of different modes of public transit, took care of her own well-being without a parent nudging (or nagging) her, and felt her world open. *And*, like there was a place for her.

She came home more connected to us, to her school, *and* to the world.

This isn't born from research, it comes from student anecdotes and my own intuition. I've been in so many rooms with students who share of their jaw-dropping, heart-bursting, perspective-expanding experiences travelling, studying, volunteering, researching, and working abroad.

And schools can be conduits for this.

From organised trips—one of my grade 11 clients who through the languages program at her high school, went on an incredible journey to Switzerland. Another second-year client went to northern Ontario on a rocketry trip. Another to Canada's Atlantic Provinces that was robotics-focused. Frequently, these trips are fundraised for and subsidised in part or full to eliminate or reduce the cost for students and families.

There are so many iterations of this to encourage your learner to consider, or connect as a family about. One route is through in-service or volunteering adventures abroad. If there's learning about cultural context, intercultural awareness, and *not* going anywhere to be a "saviour," if there's a need and an opportunity, doing service-related work in a community can be a fulfilling experience for a learner.

There can also be global experiences *at home*. Like language meetups. If your child knows how to speak another language, or wants to learn, there are free virtual or in-person conversation exchanges happening just about everywhere.

Similarly, culture nights can be a way for your learner to share their customs, ancestry, and what's important to them, and learn about others. Not ones that feel tokenistic, reductionist, or voyeur-ish, but rather opportunity to stand excitedly in one's home language, customs, and ways of being. These nourish pride in one's identity, opens up the world as well as the origins and practices of others.

Hosting international students can be another way for cultivating that sense of belonging to the wider world. There are many services seeking families to offer a room, some meals, and in the early days, some navigation support. I've heard from so many households where this has had a positive impact on everyone.

Global belonging can shift a learner's sense of what's possible, of who they are, of what their big-dream hopes are, and deepen bonds with their family, friends, and school right here.

Raising welcomed learners

Belonging has so many sides and shapes to it, but no matter how near or far that connection-making is, there is a shared sense of welcome. It's like being invited or being a member of something that isn't exclusive but matters so much to your learner. And this interconnectedness, this kinship, matters profoundly to a learner's being able to keep moving towards their school commitment goals.

When a student can't find their footing or place, when they don't feel like they're welcome in their classes on school campus, when they can't find their people and allies and kin and pal, when they can't find a trusted mentor or guide, both spirit and academics suffer.

Encouraging your learner to tend to fostering connections is as important as studying well. Belonging is what helps a student stay.

Chapter Fourteen

Co-Regulation for the Win

A lovely meme came my way not long ago, with waves and a boat and a phrase that went something like, *when their storms meet our calm*. That's precisely what this chapter takes aim at—the ways that parents can becalm, settle, and ultimately co-regulate their learners. No matter the *content* or *why* of a learner's upset, parents can, through their breath and bodies, serve as a steadying presence and salve.

Co-regulation? What's the "co" mean?

I know there's (a *lot* of) talk around self-regulation in education circles. Let's start there.

A learner's self-regulation has to do with them being able to take care of—or "manage"—their personal or internal aspects of learning, like paying attention, their emotional reactions, awareness of their thoughts or rumination, and staying on top of appropriate behavior.

Self-regulation includes things like goal-setting and schedule-setting, self-monitoring and adapting to the environment including changes in it, and heeding and incorporating feedback.

It's about a student being aware of and modulating their thinking, feeling, impulses, and behaviour. Particularly in light of the context they're in. Think of it as internal control.

What's a little bit flawed in the languaging of "self-regulation?" The heavy emphasis of the "self."

It's not "wrong." It's not "bad." It just begs questions about over-focus on the individual being distinctly in charge of all of their internal states, and it also sounds a little bit like containment. As in, don't get too loud, don't feel too much, don't over-react, don't …, don't …, don't ….

And, while behaviour in a class is important, crucially so, self-regulation speaks only to a part.

This isn't a book on teaching; it isn't from the educator's perspective. (That book's coming!) My desire here is to support parents. What grandparents, chosen family, extended family, and mentors can do to help keep their student in their orbit more well.

Thus, that "co."

We are each deeply impacted by the company we're amidst, by the surroundings we're in. So, where self-regulation infers a student harnessing or minimising their emotions and actions *on their own*, making it seems like soothing, calming, and focusing is exclusively an inside job, co-regulation recognises the power of relationships and the help that surrounds a learner.

I am *not* inviting learners to shirk responsibility. I am *not* denying a learner's agency. They are in charge. It's just that they're in charge…*and* in relationships…*that are also* in contexts.

Co-regulation honours that we individuals interact and influence each other's emotions, actions, and responses.

What else does co-regulation look like? Listening actively, empathising palpably, validating emotions, suggesting micro-interventions, and ultimately sharing the experience of or recommending a variety of coping strategies.

Back to our learners' storms meeting our calm.

I'm not suggesting that we can't be our full selves either. I don't want any parent to take away that they're "not allowed" to be frustrated, angry, sad, or unavailable. That they can't be *un*calm.

And it's not just about storms. Co-regulation is also uplifting our learners when they need encouragement, cheering them on when it's our excitement, enthusiasm, and celebratory energy they need. Comfort, reassurance, motivation, keenness—these are all forms of co-regulating tacks we can bring.

What's at the heart of co-regulation? The interconnection *of* heart. It's possible through relationships that comprise trust, care, attentive listening, and available presence.

My aim here is to share strategies for families that can support their children. Nothing denied, pushed down, not allowed. But rather an ecosystem that's honoured.

Co-regulating elementary learners

Doing this work of bringing down the energy (or lifting it up) can be a beautiful teaching from parent to child from early on. It might be fleeting, it might be full of wiggle at the get go, but beginning to help co-build a coping toolbox with them that includes ways to use the breath—these are lifelong lessons that you're seed-planting.

Play, fun, using all the senses, turning to imagination, keeping it short, and managing our expectations as parents are all what helps make anything new likelier to work.

Why does breathing work? And what does using the breath *work* for?

Breathing exercises stimulate parasympathetic nervous system activation. This is the gateway to our bodies' in-built "rest and digest" response—the becalmed, alert, grounded state we can experience in contrast to the mobilised, ready-to-go, "on" sympathetic response. From this parasympathetic perspective, breathing slows our heart rate, reduces blood pressure, decreases tension in our muscles, and amplifies that *well* and relaxed feeling.

Breathing exercises also reduce stress hormones and the correlating anxiety and agitation; boost our heart rate variability, which is the kind of resilience and flexibility in intervals between our heart beats, a sign of nervous system function, including emotional regulation; and, increase oxygen intake and flow throughout the body, lowering stress.

What kinds of breathing exercises can you try alongside your elementary-aged learner?

Belly breathing

Lie down on your backs on the floor, couch, or bed with or nearby your learner. Encourage placing one hand on their heart, the other on their belly. Why? To connect the physicality of a racing heart, and the more etheric tenderness of a feeling heart, to the deeply calming, regulatory capacity of our breathing, which we can feel in our bellies.

This breathing approach is the simplest of all—simply have them breathe into their belly, even asking them to feel not just their belly rise and fall with inhalations and exhalations, but for even more tactile support, having them breathe into that hand.

Belly breathing can be further enhanced by placing a special stone or object on their belly instead of their hand, and having your learner place their focus on the up and down of the stone on their tummy with each inhale and exhale.

This can be practised together before a homework session, before bed, or when a learner is feeling agitated or unfocused.

You can both inhale and exhale through your nose, or to experiment, try breathing in through your nose and out through your mouth.

Elevator breathing

Whether lying down or sitting up, be alongside your child, encouraging as much comfort as possible.

In this exercise, describe to your learner that you will be riding the breath elevator together. Start by inhaling in through the nose and directing intention to the region of the heart, that's the first floor. Then, on the same inhale, breathe into the solar plexus, the place between the heart and belly. Finally, still on the same inhale, send breath into your belly, the third floor. So, it's like one-third of an inhalation to the first floor (heart), second-third of the inhale to the second floor (solar plexus), and the final third of breathing in (belly). From there, you exhale, floor by floor, in reverse. Let a third out riding from the belly to the solar plexus floor, then a third out from solar plexus to heart, and the last third from the heart out the nose. In: nose to heart, heart to solar plexus, solar plexus to belly. Out: belly to solar plexus, solar plexus to heart, heart out through the nose. This can be practised anytime, anywhere.

Rose / Candle Breath

This is an upright breathing exercise, and a lovely one to do side-by-side.

Here, you can ask your learner to work with either the image of a rose (or any fragrant flower) *or* the image of a candle. They come to the same thing, but allow for some choice.

Whether flower or candle, you can have your learner raise one finger in the air, just to begin with, and imagine that they are inhaling through their nose the wonderful aroma of a beautiful flower. Or, that they are inhaling as if to prepare for blowing out a candle.

Then, at the end of the inhalation, the move from nose breathing to a long, slow breath through their mouth but with pursed lips. In the imagery of the flower, they're to imagine just fluttering the petals, instead of letting the breath gush out and knock the petals to the ground. In the case of the candle, same idea, but that they blow the candle out and gently send the smoke to the opposite side of the room.

Inhale through the nose, long, extended exhale through the mouth with rounded lips.

This can be helpful in meeting overwhelm in your learner.

Sister to breathing exercises are mindfulness practices. These can also start in the elementary grades, if not before. There's now ample and robust research around mindfulness activities supporting focus, creativity, and regulation.

"Mindfulness" is a word we might now encounter daily. It's used, perhaps, to the point of extreme. It's not a cure-all, but it is a superbly helpful skill and mode of being. We can't necessarily *live* there, but we can visit, often.

So what is it?

Mindfulness is described in many ways. As the pause between a thing happening and our response to it. As directed focus. As deep awareness. As expansive attention. As moment-by-moment paying attention. As single-minded presence.

Mindfulness is included when we do breathing exercises. How could it not be? We are, quite literally, minding our breath.

Breath is often central to mindfulness practices because it's so ready-at-hand. It's no cost, always available. It requires nothing other than turning our concentration from all of the outside, external sensory input—all that's charging towards us in every minute if not second—to our breath. The full sensation, from the inhale, moment of break or grace at the end of the exhale, then as we release all that air out, and again that momentary gap before the next inhale.

I'm including this here because mindfulness practices have a direct impact on academic experience and performance. How could it not? Mindfulness changes all aspects *called upon* for learning, from focus to clear-thinking to calm in the face of what could be overwhelming tasks.

There are lots of mindfulness exercises that aren't breath focused, and likewise do wonders for that "regulatory" quality we're seeing. Not in the sense of control, but in the sense of *agency*. As in, we can *do* something about our emotional states. And can with the support, nudging, and alongsideness of their family or chosen family participating too.

Co-regulating high school learners

The breathing and mindfulness activities above can be just as effective and relevant, and interesting, for older learners.

But we can also tap into their growing sophistication by adding complexity for both resonance and physiological and psychological impact.

One thing I always keep in mind for high schoolers is how much they're holding. All the body stuff *plus* the social stuff *plus* the academic stuff *plus* increased household responsibility stuff *plus* first jobs stuff *plus* future-thinking stuff, like further schooling or more substantial work.

So, mindfulness can, when offered as a nudge, role-modelled by families, and given without expectations, come as a relief to learners who are carrying what sometimes feels like the weight of the world for them.

The academic pressures that secondary school students face cannot be diminished. Those, "where are you going to go to college?" questions pick up in frequency, as does the, "what are you going to be when you grow up?" It's a lot. Reducing stress is a huge win from these soothing practices.

Also supported are students' capacities for concentration. With all the tech gadgetry and digital distraction, there's a daily onslaught of competition for our learners' attention. This co-regulatory work, alongside you or their peers, can help sturdy their skills at controlling and directing their attention, finding ways to anchor their focus when it's flitting.

There is also a kind of optimisation that happens for students. These practices help learners think through and create from a place of centredness, connection, and ground, instead of adrenaline, high pressure, last-minute, and panic.

Not a day goes by without a news report about student mental health. Mindful interventions are now a mainstay of psychological resilience work. These practices can support self-awareness, reduced worry, and, emotional regulation.

Back to that "co," why not leave all this for the learner to do on their own? They can! But, they might also, in their adolescence, not only still need to have that physical, embodied support of those who most care for them, but also be interested in seeking out peer mindfulness sessions, drop-in teen yoga, or group martial arts classes.

Not to mention the poignance of being in a kind and calm relationship with your teenage learner—not the usual storyline of parent-child connection from 13-18. There's no denying or pretending away the highs and lows of the emotional landscape for this age and time. But there are also so many stunning opportunities to have harmonious moments, all the while instilling coping practices that can last a lifetime.

What can we do with our learners, or teach them and encourage them to try with a trusted pal?

2:1 Breath

This breathing exercise keeps the inhales the same length and over the duration of the practice, slowly elongates the exhale.

Being in comfort, whether that's lying down or sitting. Your learner might have the capacity to not just jump in but "warm up" a little by not doing anything, not breathing any which way, but just sinking back into their body and internal experience, transitioning from the external world they've been in.

Once ready, both you and your learner can begin by breathing in for a count of four and out for a count of four, ideally inhaling and exhaling through the nose. You can both follow a beat, like a physical or online metronome, but I would much rather it be self-derived as your count of four will slow. So, you might have different counts and that's normal.

Once you've done five or six rounds of counting in and out for four—and this is arbitrary, you can do more if it feels like it—begin to slow your exhale. This would look like breathing in for four and out for a count of five. In for four, out for five.

And to clarify, because I'm all about the "how," breathing "to a count" means using that number to take the full duration of your inhale or exhale. As in, breathing in to a count of four means it takes me 1, 2, 3, 4 to go from the beginning to the end of my exhale—I'm full of breath by the last count.

After five or six rounds—of in for 4 and out for 5, extend the exhale by one again. So, in for four, out for six. Repeat another five or six times. Then, extend again. In for four, out for seven. Stay there for a while. Then, finally, in for four, out for eight.

You've doubled your exhale—deep belly breathing, deep exhalations, deep stimulation of that parasympathetic, calming response.

This can have a strong grounding effect, so it can be great post-tests after that adrenaline surge, or if your learner is struggling to sleep worrying about all of their tasks and deadlines.

Box Breath

This is a technique that has grown in popularity such that more and more young folks know about it. And for a breathwork practice to become ubiquitous is a sign of the times! The origins of this practice are said to be from Navy Seal training, and it's sometimes called Square Breathing.

It brings in the beauty of focusing both on breath and on count; two anchor access points.

The basic framework is that you breathe in for a count of four, hold the breath for a count of four, exhale for a count of four, then hold again for four.

You can do these to-a-count breaths with a metronome or beat, or count them internally, which is what I prefer, as everyone's breathing rhythm is different and there's no need to feel pressure to breathe faster or more slowly.

Let's try!

Alongside your learner, either sitting upright on a meditation cushion or slumped on a chair, or lying down on the floor or a bed, come home to your body. What does that mean? Turn the outside world off, and inhabit the inner one—healing from all that sensory stimulus that surrounds us.

Once settled, take a few clearing breaths.

Slowly inhale into your belly to a four-count so that you reach the end of your exhale on the four. Now hold your breath for that same pacing of a four-count. Within releasing the air all at once, exhale for a four-count, reaching the end of your exhale on the four. Then again, hold your breath for that four-count.

Repeat this box or square. In for four, hold for four, out for four, hold for four. Repeat. Repeat. Repeat.

You can do this with a timer set for 5 or 10 minutes, or for a certain number of boxes, which might be a bit more difficult to keep track of.

Before you jump out of the practice, move from the counting breath to your own natural breath. There's quite a feeling when you drop the count and it's worth savouring. Enjoy the freedom of your inhales and exhales. And, take notice of the state of your mind, and whether there have been any shifts—then, after, ask your learner what they experienced.

Lovingkindness Meditation

To direct the big emotions of adolescence, a lovingkindness meditation might be a good fit. This practice has us wish not just ourselves well, but those we love, and ultimately the whole world. It is a tenderising activity and can bring you and your learner closer.

You can find a free guided lovingkindness meditation to follow, or you or your highschooler can lead with a prepared script—there are many free online ones. I'll give you a very simple version that you can both read through, get the gist of, and then practise silently together. But my best suggestion is to create your own version *with* your teen. Once you've both tried this a few times, it'd be beautiful for you to come up with the phrases together, based upon what's most important to you both, and what words most resonate.

To get into things, take any position that's comfortable. Make sure your lungs have room to breathe and that your limbs are soft—as in, your arms aren't crossed across your chest, and if sitting, one leg isn't crossed over the other. An open, easy way of being in the body is ideal.

Before any formal practice, start with a transition in—settling into the bones, into the heart, into the breath. Moving the focus from the outside world to the inside one—your inhales, exhales, pulse, and body.

Once you and your learner are both feeling grounded, let's begin!

Inhale a long, slow breath. On the exhale, say the phrase silently to yourself: *may I be well.* Inhale. Exhale: *may I be safe.* Inhale. Exhale: *may I be free from inner and outer harm.* Inhale. Exhale: *may I be happy and know peace.*

Take a few inhales and exhales—long, slow.

Inhale a long, slow breath. On the exhale: *may my* ____ (the family / chosen family you're sitting with) *be well.* Inhale. Exhale: *may they be safe.* Inhale. Exhale: *may they be free from inner and outer harm.* Inhale. Exhale: *may they be happy and know peace.*

Take a few inhales and exhales—long, slow.

Inhale a long, slow breath. On the exhale: *may my closest loved ones be well.* Inhale. Exhale: *may they be safe.* Inhale. Exhale: *may they be free from inner and outer harm.* Inhale. Exhale: *may they be happy and know peace.*

Take a few inhales and exhales—long, slow.

Inhale a long, slow breath. On the exhale: *may my neighbourhood be well.* Inhale. Exhale: *may they be safe.* Inhale. Exhale: *may they be free from inner and outer harm.* Inhale. Exhale: *may they be happy and know peace.*

Take a few inhales and exhales—long, slow.

Inhale a long, slow breath. On the exhale: *may my school community be well.* Inhale. Exhale: *may they be safe.* Inhale. Exhale: *may they be free from inner and outer harm.* Inhale. Exhale: *may they be happy and know peace.*

Take a few inhales and exhales—long, slow.

Inhale a long, slow breath. On the exhale: *may my town/city be well.* Inhale. Exhale: *may they be safe.* Inhale. Exhale: *may they be free from inner and outer harm.* Inhale. Exhale: *may they be happy and know peace.*

Take a few inhales and exhales—long, slow.

Inhale a long, slow breath. On the exhale: *may this world, and all of its people, animals, trees, and plants be well.* Inhale. Exhale: *may they all be safe.* Inhale. Exhale: *may they all be free from inner and outer harm.* Inhale. Exhale: *may they all be happy and know peace.*

Take a few final inhales and exhales—as always, long, slow, unrushed.

This one would be wonderful to debrief together.

Co-regulating post-secondary learners

With your learner in post-secondary, this is a wonderful time to engage in these co-regulating practices together—with *potentially* less chance of pushback, mockery, and sarcasm!

This is the era of grown-up habits. Nuanced and sophisticated, new or on the road to enduring. Strategies for coping and thriving through the adult decades.

It's not meant to be bleak—of course adulthood is full of excitement and adventure, highs and joys. But we know, as parents, that there are pitfalls and profound hurts. Ones that require us to have a toolkit of strategies, ideally well worn, that help us tend and recover.

I'm not diminishing the very real challenges of the younger years. There are many children and young adults who face extraordinary harms and hurdles.

By the older years, we come to know that to be a human is to experience suffering. And my life's work, always, is to contribute to less of it.

These practices are, again, able to be engaged with through-out the years, but may find an extra spark with this life-stage. They ask for a little bit more capacity as they're layered or multi-stepped practices.

4-7-8 Breathing

Breathing to any kind of count can be purposefully helpful for minds that struggle to settle—which might well be everyone's. In addition to the breath, the counting is a second anchor for attention, very useful to hone attention.

In this popular breathing technique, the approach is to inhale through the nose for a four-count, hold the breath for a seven-count, and exhale through the mouth for an eight-count. That's the overarching shape.

Get comfy, sitting up or lying down, feeling supported by whatever is underneath your bodies.

You can do a check-in with your learner before getting going, asking them to share with you, or just reflect silently, how they're doing—the state of their body, mind, and heart. They can also pay attention to the quality of their breath before beginning—is it shallow or high, is it felt in the nose or the throat, is it fast or slow?

Start with a deep inhale for a count of four—again each person's "4" might be different, yet if it's helpful you can breathe to a beat. In through the nose for four. Hold then for a count of seven. Exhale for a count of eight through the mouth for eight, being mindful to not let the exhaled breath out in a gush, but slow, long, and controlled. Then repeat. Then repeat. Then repeat again.

You can do this for time, like 10 minutes, or you can do this for repetitions, like 15 rounds.

Nadi Shodhana / Alternate Nostril Breathing

This is great for regaining equilibrium or balance, clearing the mind, and restoring focus.

233

If this is new to you, I recommend going through the steps, getting sorted with the rhythm, and practising together a little bit first—like playing open-hand the first time you play a new card game.

As always, start with comfort. I've been taught this as a seated practice, which feels ideal to me, but you can experiment with lying down if sitting doesn't feel good for your or your learner's body. Find a way to sit that helps you both feel upright without being rigid, and soft in the belly with out slumping into a chair. It's a balance between up and soft, between straight and supple.

When you feel settled, relaxed, *in* your body, do a few rounds of natural inhales and exhales with attention or *intention*. Bringing that focus inwards. Finding your breath interesting. Letting that loud mental chatter ease off, even if only a little or momentarily.

Bring your right hand up palm-side in front of your face. Fold in your index and middle fingers. Extend your ring and pinky fingers.

With your right thumb, close off your right nostril. Inhale deeply into your left nostril.

With your right ring and pinky fingers, close off your left nostril. Hold your breath. Release your right thumb. Exhale through your right nostril.

With your right ring and pinky fingers still closing your left nostril, inhale deeply into your right nostril.

With your right thumb, close off your right nostril. Hold your breath. Release your right ring and pink fingers. Exhale through your left nostril.

Repeat this alternating cycle.

Thumb on right nostril, inhale deeply into left nostril.

Ring and pinky finger on left nostril, hold, release right thumb, exhale right nostril.

Inhale deeply into right nostril, thumb on right nostril, hold, release ring and pinky ringer on left nostril, exhale left nostril.

Repeat.

Do this for a number of rounds. Beyond just getting the hang of it; get into a flow.

One variation is to uncurl your index and middle fingers and place them in the middle of your forehead. This might feel even more clarifying for the mind.

After you've completed however many rounds or however much time feels right, perhaps 10 rounds, perhaps 5 minutes, perhaps longer, lower your hand and breathe naturally.

This is a wonderful practice to share reflections on afterwards. What's the mind like? What's your breathing like? (The reason I like to do this sitting is that I find it really clears the nose!)

This requires so much focus and coordination, and is so potent, that it can be a good match during times of worry or overwhelm. It can bring learners (and parents!) right back into the present moment, more resourced, feeling grounded again.

Contemplative Reading

Post-secondary students do *so* much reading. Before class, after class, their notes. Articles, chapters, case studies, papers, textbooks, novels. To be a college or university student is to be reading *a lot*. Most of that reading is done for a specific purpose—for an assignment, presentation, studying. There isn't often much pleasure, or if there is, it's accidental.

Contemplative reading is like the *opposite* of reading for school—that said, I *wish* that reading for school felt full of pleasure, delight, ease, connection, curiosity.

Have your learner borrow a book from your local library, or purchase a used or new one, that is specifically meant to be read slowly. In other words, their favourite graphic novel series or fantasy tome may not be so suitable for this. The aim here is to read slowly. Like a line, paragraph, or page.

This could be poetry. This could be a book of inspirational quotes. This could be a spiritual book. Anything that feels full of insight. There can be illustrations or not.

And, it can be a book written for this purpose, *or not*. It's in the intention you and your learner bring to it that will make it an appropriate book. Anything that feels like it can impart wisdom. That feels like a delicious mouthful. That feels like it needs a minute. That lends itself to going slowly in contrast to that quickness that drives most of our days.

This activity is seemingly straightforward. Be together as a family community, read the passage or portion slowly aloud, and then share interpretations or how you'll bring it into the day. My stepdaughter bought me a set of mindfulness cards, set up like a tarot deck, for Mother's Day one year. And though we've been through the pack several times over, almost every morning we read one at breakfast time.

They serve as a small reminder. They have us listen in, with ears and hearts. And though the busyness and goings-on of the day will inevitably take over, there's a chance that through continuous practice a seed gets planted and tended to.

It's a different way to read, and to listen. A mindful pushback against what oftentimes feels like the onslaught of our days.

And, to read *together*, brings a different quality—a sharedness in mindful intent.

A Note of Thanks

It's too beautiful that this practice now has so much scientific backing to it: the gratitude letter.

The process is to write a letter of appreciation to someone accessible (or not), living (or not), then give (and read) the letter. If they're not available for any reason, you can read the letter to someone who knew them, or someone important to you that you can share the significance and meaning of that relationship with.

Key elements are to focus on their qualities, their impact on you, and the nature and effect of the relationship. And, to spend time absorbing the positive ripples after sharing the letter (in whatever form).

Let's expand this gratitude letter practice.

It doesn't have to be in letter form. Sure, there's something about creating and receiving something literally hand-crafted. The lettering, the stationary. But, it's no less meaningful if it comes in other modalities.

Creating and receiving something hand-crafted is wonderful, but the gratitude letter doesn't have to be in letter form. It can come in other modalities that are just as meaningful.

You can send a thank you text. In fact, I ask my post-secondary students to do this—in class. If they can send a thank you text then and there. And I challenge them to have the first text they send each day be one of gratefulness.

But it can also be an audionote. These are my favourite. One of my dear friends and collaborators, she and I send loving voice texts to each other—often!

237

It can be a post-it—these are what I write my kids and sneak them into places for them to stumble upon. It can be a hand-made postcard.

The format doesn't *really* matter.

It's about the deep and lovely consideration of another and your bond.

What if you and your learner intentionally shared these with each other. What would you write? What would you want to highlight about what you appreciate about them, about how their presence and way of being has changed your life, about what you notice and cherish about them? And, imagine receiving that from your learner?

Consider making this a full family / chosen family practice! Notice, most stunningly, the after-impact of this. The good feelings that not only emerge during but *after*. This is where all that research comes into being.

It is a balm, it is a sweetness. I'm eager for you to give it a try! Is breathwork, are mindfulness practices, for everyone? Nope. For some folks, these can agitate, these can disturb a sense of safety, these can trigger. The hope in presenting so many different approaches is that perhaps one or two might feel safe, useful, and good. But underneath any offering, whether about emotional regulation or any other learning strategy in the book—encourage your learner to trust their intuition, their gut, their inner wisdom, their body's feedback. If it doesn't feel good, don't do it.

All of these can be done solo by your learner, but having your body and theirs both engaging in the practice of soothing the internal systems is a bonus. Why is the *togetherness* of these practices so encouraged here? In addition to the profound comfort one body can provide another when in trusted relationship, through proximity, there's the rich opportunity for reflection and processing.

After any exercise or practice, you can share your experiences—from the wrestling with distraction to the glimpses of peace to the big, relaxed yawns at the same time. You can ask how they're feeling now as compared with before—being sure not to "I told you so" or shame those before feels. You can ask how they feel in their body—like in their jaw or stomach. You can reflect back what their face looks like now—perhaps softer. You can share your somatic sensations, where your mind and heart are at now, what you feel ready for. A lovely addition to any of these approaches is to take a temperature, pulse, or weather check before and after. Not literally the temperature, your pulse, or the outside weather, but the inside heat or coolness, racing or slowness, storms or clear skies.

What can grow is an understanding not just of oneself, but of each other. An exposing of what stresses us out and what gives us relief. And, indeed, what a sweet relief to be in that parasympathetic, open-hearted, becalmed state *together*.

Raising (co)regulated learners

Students can do any of these practices on their own—and I hope they do, I hope they take their experiences with you as their trusted mindfulness sidekick and engage in these on their own whenever they need. And they can also contemplate or journal their before-after feelings independently as well.

In the presence and company of each other, they're also learning regulation *from you*. They're watching and experiencing you melt, relax, and cope. What a life gift—to see one's parents move from stressed, in charge, and on the go to a state of ease!

Perhaps most of all, togetherness emotional regulation practices add one more piece to your bond. In doing these kinds of exercises together there is a poignant honesty of you both, of us all, being tender, fragile, often-hurt, often-stress bodies. How normal. How common. How human.

And that relational, being-together, *human* piece is really the crux of co-regulation. Bodies doing their best to come home to themselves alongside one another.

Chapter Fifteen

Improve GPA with a Nap

Pose the question to any learner, "how are you?" and what will the response likely be?

"Stressed."

"Busy."

And, above all, "tired."

Students are tired. Almost all of the time. (So are, I want to add, parents.) Families too. Almost everyone I know will say that they're exhausted to some, or a great, extent.

It's no wonder, really. Students are *in it*. Piled up, and piled on, assignments and assessments—to plan for, chip away at, and hand in. Along with all the inner demons they encounter in doing those assignments and assessments—procrastination, distraction, perfectionism, amotivation—each borrowing capacity and inner-resourcing. There are big school expectations—doing well, so much so that if post-secondary is the aim, well enough to secure a spot, or a scholarship. Students are immersed in all kinds of co- or extra-curricular engagements—at school, out of school, music and art and athletic and STEM and languages and community.

Add to this the many students that have long commutes to school.

And part-time jobs, which are sometimes erratic shifts, or at very early or very late times of day. Some students have multiple jobs, full-time jobs, or businesses they're running.

Students have injuries they're trying to heal from. They have disabilities that require extra energy in the form of: time to get to class, particularly on inclement weather days; time to schedule aides and assistants; time to get new or updated medical documentation and paperwork; time for specialist appointments, medical tests, treatments; time for medication side effect recovery, including additional fatigue or inability to sleep; time to meet with, for example in post-secondary, their disability consultant or academic accommodation facilitator, to check-in around courses and assessment expectations, and advocating for specific requirements.

Students have community commitments like prayer time, big family gatherings, rituals and celebrations, customs and rhythms that need honouring.

Students have basic life to-dos like picking up a younger sibling, running household errands, volunteering, helping a friend.

And, students have full social lives, both in-person and virtually. Hangouts, meet-ups, study groups, movies, videogames, coffee, shopping, parties. The realm of the social is its own full courseload.

Each of these take time to do, they take bandwidth to plan for and schedule in or around.

The key is "capacity." You'll notice, more frequently, a shift from conversations about or the language of "time management" but rather *"capacity* management." Which is really an emphasis on inner-resourcing. On how we can reclaim, rebuild, rejuvenate some of the energy we expend.

Often, these are overlooked. Back to that "what counts" as productive. Or to what's considered a subtractive takeaway from a schedule or an additive. This is starting to amplify, but we're not quite there.

Schoolwork is often seen as something that "comes first." That's "top priority." That needs to be planned around, instead of planning schoolwork around health-promoting activities.

Students' lives are, generally, ruled by teachers' deadlines. So, how can students, whether in K–12 or post-secondary, who have very little agency or choice or power to say "no" or "I'll get to that later" feel *less* exhausted and *more* rested? And, why is rest important to academic success?

In all the exhaustion—in families and chosen families, in the school pressures and demands—the main message students are given is to keep going, stay up, do what it takes—to work "harder," study "more."

There's a "you'll get through this." Or, "buck up." Or, "it's only fatigue." Or, "think of it like a rite of passage."

But that working "harder" and studying "more" simply add to and compound fatigue, and lead to burnout. And learners *don't* actually have to experience the burnout their parents do.

What's not shared with students? How nutrition, hydration, sleep, and rest directly impact academic performance—they're not "nice-to-haves," they're essential for sustainable success.

No longer does the pushing-through-at-all-cost mentality have to reign supreme. No longer do students have to feel like they're in a zombie movie when they go to school, going through the motions, bleary-eyed, sleepwalking.

In this last chapter, I imagine there feels as though there's a likely rhythm—aiming to debunk or disrupt stubborn beliefs about what leads to learning success.

An A is absolutely possible by a student running themselves ragged on an assignment. Maybe a second one. Maybe a semester's worth. But to experience high performance, to confidently produce high quality work, burnout prevention is key. Running ragged course after course, year after year, isn't a sustainable strategy.

Preventing burnout is more than just to get an A.

Students often feel like they *have* to push themselves to the limit—extraordinarily late nights, extreme caffeine and sugar consumption, hour after hour slumped over a laptop. But we can shift the image and the conversation about what goes into an *enduring* A and a healthy life.

Remembering rest

Even the *word* "rest," and let's add in "ease" as well, can feel so helpful. Like a permission slip to be human. Can you feel it?

What would it feel like for our learners for us to remind them to rest? To take ease? Along with putting away their laundry, and getting their homework done, nudging them to pause and restore, what would that be like for them?

Rest is a misconflated, underrated, and seldom included part of the learning mix.

Often equated with each other, rest and sleep are assumed to be the same thing, but they're not. To rest, doesn't mean to sleep.

So what *is* rest?

Is rest watching YouTube videos between study sessions? No.

Is rest playing video games? No.

Is rest mindless scrolling? No.

Am I anti-tech? Nope!

Rest is a break from sensory input. It's a pushback against the onslaught of things to look at and listen to. It's a pause from hard cognitive work. It's a reprieve.

So why isn't gaming or taking a mindless social scroll not rest in this context? Well, they might give the impression of relaxation but they're demanding something of us; they're taking more than they're giving.

I'm really talking about active rest. Utterly and purposefully restoring. Things that *give* more than they take.

There's been a proliferation of conversation and content about rest. Lots of different things to try, to consider: "rest can look like X, or Y, or Z." But in the back of my mind is that these will be charged for, and I don't want families spending any more dollars than they truly have to, and I fear the rabbit hole around *researching* rest, that rest becomes its own tense pursuit of Googling and landing upon the "right" kind of practice or approach.

I long to make for more ease, less chaos, *less* noise, and simpler options. I want to ease the pathway for your learner, and you, to *experience* rest.

We can think of rest in two ways: rest that's still and rest that's moving.

Still Rest

Could your learner just lie on the floor for five minutes and that be rest? You bet.

245

Is that all there is to it? Could be.

Are there any other options? Heck yes!

To be sure, I sometimes just lie on the floor. Between online clients. After a virtually delivered keynote. But there are two powerful add-ons I want to share. The first is guided rest while lying down, and the second is different postures you can rest in—both promote deep rest.

This can be done solo by your learner, and you're suggesting, nudging, and feeding them the ideas. Or, better yet, together. What parent, what professional, what *human* doesn't need a little (or a lot) more rest?!

Let's start with guided restfulness while lying down. Comfortably on the floor, supporting your head with a folded thin blanket, perhaps an extra layer of clothes as we cool down as we become more restful, and pillows or a rolled-up towel under your knees to support your back. You can also do this lying on a bed, but I would discourage it if possible—your bed is deeply associated with sleep.

The aim of still rest is *not* to sleep. You and your learner might well fall asleep, it's common and normal. But the intention is to stay alert.

There are two main ways we're doing to approach this form of still rest: yoga nidra and non-sleep deep rest (NSDR).

Yoga nidra is not about movement, it's not about a sweaty stretch class, which is sometimes what gets misunderstood about the word "yoga." In the simplest definition, and I am *not* a Sanskrit speaker, it's about the relationship or union of breath and body. It might look, in your neighbourhood, that it's about lithe bodies in pretzel shapes. That's just one small sliver of what yoga *can* mean, but it's not the heart of it.

Yoga *nidra* is yogic sleep. It's an altered state of consciousness that's between sleeping and wakefulness, and it's restful beyond compare.

You could absolutely take a yoga nidra class in a studio—I have, and it's delicious. But you can also pop on a guided yoga nidra meditation from a free app or via web-searching and be transported.

Yoga nidra is a carefully considered sequence of bringing a person's attention to different body parts, releasing tension, and sinking deeper, layer by layer, into rest. There's often an intention-setting element, there can be guided imagery. And your best bet is to proactively find a track or two with a voice that feels soothing, a routine that feels manageable, for a duration that works for you and your learner.

A newer iteration comes from Dr. Andrew Huberman, Stanford University professor and creator of The Huberman Lab, called NSDR—non-sleep deep rest—his broadly accessible version of yoga nidra. The logic is the same. In NSDR, there is a focus on the breath, and on a scan of the body.

Whatever the form, these are deeply nourishing, non-nap, active rest breaks.

If you or your learner *do* fall asleep, that's okay!

The other key way I'm going to suggest engaging in active rest is through physical postures.

These are borrowed from what's called Restorative Yoga. When you picture yoga, it might not be stillness that immediately comes to mind. Yoga is often narrowly understood in its current manifestations, particularly in my part of the world. I love a good, big-movement, sweaty yoga class, but let's slow things right down to the point of not moving at all.

Years ago, I feel very lucky to have participated in a Restorative Yoga Teacher Training when I was doing a larger, year-long yoga teaching certification course. What so moves me about Restorative is that it purposefully invites deep release, ease, equilibrium, and replenishment in the body. That's the point.

Bones settle into their joints. Our parasympathetic system kicks in, that rest and digest mode of being. Our clenched places let go a little. It is sublime.

The first posture you can try is called—and I find this so poignant—"constructive rest pose." I remember the first time I heard that pose name. Constructive rest. I couldn't believe it. Like "rest on purpose."

And not necessarily (or at all) rest for more work, more productivity, more doing afterwards. Rather, I think of it as rest, on purpose, because we need it. Because our bodies and beings long for it.

For sure, upped capacity is a natural result, but I'm not suggesting to rest for the sole purpose of being able to do more. That's just a natural consequence.

How to *do* constructive rest?

You and your learner can, on a yoga mat or rug, or even a couch or bed, lie down on your backs with your knees bent. Fold a blanket for under your head—not a pillow that lifts your head up too much, just something low and padded. Your feet stay on the floor, sole down. And the bed is a very natural one—your knee-bend is like an upside-down V, that's about the shape and angle of it.

From there, knees fall inwards so that they're resting against each other. Why? So that you don't even have to exert the effort to hold your knees up. That's how easeful this is meant to be! Let them lean in and support each other.

Arms can be outstretched, in a cactus shape, by your sides palm-up, or with one hand on your heart, another on your belly.

This pose invites a settling in. The body can reclaim alignment. The mind can slow. From here, it could be a few minutes of following the breath, or a mantra of "peace" on the inhale and "ease" on the exhale, or any other words that resonate.

Try this for 3 minutes, or longer, then debrief together!

Another Restorative Yoga posture to try is legs-up-the-wall, or *viparita karani*. It's my personal favourite. I've even written a whole academic chapter on it!

For this one, you'll need access to a clear portion of a wall, just about four feet of empty wall from the ground up, and about two feet wide. So, choose a space that is free of paintings or a big plant pot on the floor.

Here as well, you'll lie on the floor. A yoga mat or towel or blanket can be useful. And again, something thin and folded to rest under your head will make things more comfortable.

To start, have you and your learner sit on the floor *beside* the wall with your right hip touching the wall. To put this differently, your seat is on the floor, your hip might be by a baseboard or where the floor and wall meet, and your right arm will be touching the wall.

Lean to the left and allow your right hip to lift off the ground— it likely won't touch the wall anymore. Place both hands on the ground by your left hip.

Use your hands to lower your torso to the ground and as you do, thoughtfully swing your legs up the wall.

Now, your back will be on the floor, ideally on that mat or thin, soft fabric, your bottom will be a little bit away from the wall, and your heels will be touching the wall.

You can scoot yourself closer to the wall if you wish, but it's not necessary. Or, if your hamstrings are tight, you can scoot a little further away from the wall. Your heels will still be on the wall.

Place the folded blanket underneath your head, and rest in this position for 3, 6, or 9 minutes.

There are some variations you can try for this legs–up-the-wall pose:

- You can elevate your hips by placing a half-bolster, if you have one, or a folded towel, under your sacrum.
- You can use a strap, belt, or scarf around your calves to keep your legs close together, but not tight, prioritising such ease that you don't have to use any effort to keep your legs from rotating outwards.
- You can use an eye mask; you could even use weighted bags or heavy bags of rice, on your lower belly, on your hands, or if someone can help, on the soles of your feet (just make sure it's secure and won't roll off on your head!).

If your legs get a pins and needles sensation, you can tense each calf, first one, then the other, like an alternating pulse. Or, you can bring your legs down.

This inversion is such a powerful technique to invite stillness and settledness in the body.

Moving Rest

The other day, one of my daughters said to me, before walking herself the 15 minutes to volunteer at her dance studio, "Mom, are you sure you can't walk me up today? It's really un-fun to walk by myself."

On my end, I was booked into a meeting. Now, if she had expressed any safety concerns, you bet I would've moved or cancelled whatever I had in my calendar.

But, to provide the fun? Nope.

It's not that I was unsympathetic. It *is* fun to walk together. Or do anything together. I'm an all-in, fun-loving parent. But, that no-fun is super important too.

In fact, even if she had nowhere she needed to go, I would still recommend a no-fun walk. No talking, no music, no phone, just walking.

Why?

Because that's where the magic is.

When we walk in nature, or move in the ways our bodies can, all kinds of things happen. Our capacity for creative thinking, connection-making, and innovative problem-solving open up. And it's not necessary that you need to *hold* the problem—an essay-topic, a math equation, an interpersonal conflict—as you walk. It's just what happens underneath—all kinds of processing.

On this *restful* walk, we're doing to do things a little bit differently.

Maybe your learner is open to doing this with you. Or, maybe you'll let them know about this as a technique they can do, or you can model it through doing it yourself and then reporting back.

Have them, or go together, walk in silence. It can be short, a few blocks. If going together, you can walk side-by-side, walk one behind the other, or go in different but equal distances, like loops going in opposite directions meeting back up at the starting point.

The pace of walking is slower than going on an errand. In many ways, this is purposeful rest, it is not purposeful walking. There is nowhere to get to, nowhere to go.

So, what do you "do" on these walks?

Find an *internal* point to focus on. An *internal* point. Like what? Your footsteps. You can focus on the movement and shape and arc of each footstep as you lift one foot and then place it down, then the other side. You can focus on the nature of walking, like how there's equilibrium of a sort but there's also an always *off*-balance quality to being in-motion. You could focus on your legs or your arms, without changing their stride, gait, or swing, just feeling into your limbs. You could focus on your belly, not clenching, just feeling into what your belly is up to. You could focus on your pulse or your breath, noticing how they quicken. Or, you could absolutely focus on the external, as it passes. A bird in a tree, a flutter of leaves, a nest—whatever you encounter on your walk.

For sure, it could be mostly *human*-made things you notice. Houses. Cars (and vanity licence plates). Sidewalks, and cracks in them. But as much as possible, even if nature is scarce in your neighbourhood, see what you *can* see—or hear, or sense—of nature. Cloud formations. Bird song. Rain. And it's not just what we can see or hear. It could be a breeze on your skin, or the sound of wind. It could be the feeling of snow on your cheeks.

Now, not at all assuming this is available, but if you can find a labyrinth near your house, please go! Sometimes, these are painted in wading pools in local parks so that that folks can walk them during the rest of the year, or whenever the pool isn't filled. Sometimes, they're in bigger naturalised areas. Sometimes, they're built into nature. Sometimes, these are right in the densest of urban areas. In my city, there are three relatively nearby—one in each of these types of environments. This can be lovely for mindful walking without thinking about where you're "going next." Don't worry if you don't have access to one as there are no-cost, available right-where-you-are options.

Stretching is a good one. I don't have any particular routine to suggest—and if you wanted a set sequence, there are loads online. A screen-free stretch session guided by your own bodies, is best.

I'd like both you and your learner to stretch gently, in ways that counteract the positions your bodies are usually in. For example, as an educator who spends a lot of time teaching, speaking, and writing online, I often find myself hunched over. Others might lean over a lot during the day due to their occupations, like those who are osteopaths and massage therapists.

To stretch in this instance is to think about the antidotes to those habitual shapes we're in. A student is most often at a desk writing, using a laptop, reading. To open up the spaces that have been crunched or hunched could look like:

- Stretching the pecs: stand at a wall with a cactus arm, place on a wall, and the rotate away from the wall so that there's a gentle stretch across your pectoral muscles; stay for as many breaths as you wish, deeply inhaling and exhaling, then switch sides.
- Stretching the quads: stand at a wall for balance, catch the top of your ankle with your hand behind you, and breathe into your quad as you find the right amount of sensation; stay, stretch, breathe, switch.
- Stretching the hip flexors: stand with your feet off-set like you were going to do a lunge, shorten you stance just a little, lunge slightly, but instead of the focus being placed

on sinking deep as if you were strength-training, don't go down very far and instead tuck your pelvis under so that you can feel sensation in your hip flexor; stay, stretch, breathe, switch.

- Stretching the calves: using the lowest step if you have stairs in your house, or with your foot on a block or big sturdy book, or standing close-up against the wall, stretch out the calf muscles either one at a time or both at once.
- Stretching the forearms: with arms outstretched in front of you, shoulder-height, palms down, point your fingers downwards and breathe; then rotate your arms so that your palms are facing up, now point your fingers down again.

These stretches can feel delicious. They're a different kind of stretch than those we might do to cool down after exercising. These are slow, we're in our regular clothes, they're short, they're in the middle of a study session or workday, they're quiet, they're breath focused, and they're meant to be slow and subtle *as* a rest practice.

Finally, you can shake your body. This is a third moving rest suggestion.

You can start by bouncing your heels up and down. Do that for a minute. Then, you can, with feet flat, bounce at your knees. Another minute. These aren't squats, just bounces. Keep this moving upwards, letting your torso and shoulders bounce too. Another minutes. Next, bring in your arms, and shake them. One more minute. Shake your hands and wrists. A minute. Take a whole-body shake. One last minute.

Then stop. What does it feel like in your body? You can put one hand on belly and one on heart, or not at all, and have your arms by your sides. The post-shake key here is to, sink into some feedback from the body.

There's an aliveness that's replenished when we shake. It's very simple—the shortest instructions—because our bodies really know how to do this. Shake in any way that makes sense to you. Blood's flowing, heart's pumping, things are moving.

Shaking often makes people feel silly. Self-conscious. Awkward. So, if you really can't do this together and feel like you can let go, have it be a seed that's planted for you each to do solo.

Or, maybe, there's no self-consciousness at all, and you can shake in full silliness together, no holding back!

What would happen if these still or moving rest practices became woven into the tool and technique repertoire of learning strategies that your student could incorporate during the day?

Instead of an energy drink, instead of a sweet treat "to keep going," instead of a fifteenth YouTube video on "a break," if your learner was able to hear and heed the deep feedback underneath—for rest, for shutting down the sensory input for a few minutes. What would the experience of doing their work be like? What would the *quality* of their work be like? And, how would they *feel*, not just as a student, but as a *person*?

Centering sleep

Given that there are whole books—and book series—written on the science of sleep, not to mention podcasts, academic journal articles, and TED Talks galore, my contributions will be minimal. But what I wish to offer to you and your learner is how central it is *for learning*.

Students face a murky path with sleep.

There's encouragement to be well and rested for morning classes, and then there are evening parties and late-night study sessions.

There's mention from parents and family members how tired a learner may look or seem, yet there's the language of "all-nights" that are sometimes prized and bragged about.

What I find curious is how seldom we hear from learners, "I'm rested" or "I'm feeling so healthy right now" or "I've got a lot of energy these days" when students are asked how they are. Back to where we started: it's almost always some variation of "tired."

What are learners to do when there are temptations galore, yet day after day of requirements that require full focus and sustained effort?

What are chosen families to do when their nagging doesn't help?

My feeling is that we make clear to learners, sleep is often the missing part to getting that A.

I'm hopeful that this is enough of a mic drop moment, enough of a provocative claim, that your learners perk up and take notice.

When to sleep

The best advice from a friend that I've ever heard was for sleep to become the fixed point in our day such that everything else fits around it.

When I heard this, it felt revolutionary. Now, looking back, I wonder how I ever did anything else.

At the time of encountering this teaching, I was working full-time, had two small children, was doing my PhD, and was creating thriving-related interventions for learners. Like you, I had lots going on.

Every night, after putting my children to bed, I would work on getting a reading done or chip away at writing a grad school paper. I would go to sleep when I was physically finished, not when I was finished reading or writing my paper.

Then, I'd sleep until my alarm woke me up. My alarm never changed. It didn't shift according to how late I went to bed. It was always 5:30am.

I used to dread the sound of my alarm. Getting out of bed felt like peeling myself away from it. When I finally sat up, my eyes felt gritty, my body tired and achy, and all I wanted was to lie back down. But, I ignored it every day, thinking, "once I get started...." A cup of coffee helped, and when the kids woke up full of energy, the rest of the day flew by.

But wow was I ever tired.

Exactly like so many students.

Here's the advice I received from a friend:

1. Determine how much sleep you need, without justification. (My colleague, who is now a friend, used to say she needed 10 hours of sleep without any apologies. Over time, she realised that this wasn't just what she found most nourishing, but what she actually needed to feel and be well.)
2. Identify your wake-up. (Whatever your life looks like—daycare drop-off, long commute, work from home, meal prep—figure out your rise time to make your life go.)
3. Count backwards. (So, if your wake-up time is 7am and your sleep need is 10 hours, then 9pm is lights-out bedtime.)

9pm might sound early to some, but it's accurate. The friend I mentioned, goes to bed at 9pm because to go to bed later than that is denying her body what it needs to be clear headed, to stay healthy, to have even moods and not be snappy with others, and to be energetic and productive.

It's so simple and such obvious advice, but I hadn't been living that way at all.

And, she puts this advice beautifully: work has to fit around sleep, not the other way around.

In other words, sleep comes first.

SLEEP COMES FIRST.

Since then, no matter the deadline, I've not allowed work to borrow from my bedtime.

Like every learning strategy, it's about the how. And sleeping is no different.

Learners, like us parents and professionals, can experience a lot of challenges around sleep. But there are ways we can support ourselves and our learners in having a better night's sleep more often, and regularly. (If there's insomnia going on, medication-impacted sleep, mental health challenges that are making regular sleep patterns difficult, please see a trusted health provider.)

The first is what happens *before* bedtime.

There are two key elements that we can do during the day that are in direct support of good sleep.

- Immersing in morning light. This helps with our circadian rhythm. I have had one of my post-secondary learner-clients go on a morning walk or jog in a nearby greenspace after he shared with me that he has a hard time making it to his early morning class, which revealed he had a hard time waking up, which revealed he had a hard time sleeping well throughout the night.

- Moving during the day. Sometime in your learner's day, well clear of bedtime, encourage them (and you too?) to get some movement in. It can be outdoors or in, it can be strength or cardio related, it can take the shape and rhythm of anything that feels fun and uplifting. Movement and sleep are interconnected, and just about two of the most healthful things we can do. Daytime movement will help with nighttime sleep.

As we go throughout our days, we build our sleep drive—as the day goes on, we get sleepier. That's what we want to have happen. We want to move, play, think, work, connect in healthful ways that increase our tiredness so that at the end of the day, we're able to fall asleep well. Movement should happen throughout, windows of work should happen throughout, time to connect and experience uplift should happen throughout.

Aim to keep away from the sleep disturbers. Late caffeine, overindulging in sugar, some or a lot of alcohol, heavy meals before bed, tech pre-bedtime, too hot a room—these are all things that can get in the way of a good night's sleep.

What we do *right* before bed matters too! It's often called a buffer zone—the window prior to lights out sets up our sleep well too. It's so that we're not zooming straight from work into slumber. It's a gap between the fast and the hard stop of sleep—a winding, slowing, gearing down.

This is a humane approach. In a buffer zone, some learners might respond well to a warm bath, or to a craft, or to playing a musical instrument (acoustic!), or to reading for pleasure, or to slow stretches. Non-work, non-"productive,"quiet and calm.

It's an *easing* into bed. A buffer between the workday—and it's pace, stress, demands, to-dos, and often, feelings of not-enoughs—to recuperative sleep.

Sometimes, learners can fall asleep well, especially after all of these adjustments, but might wake up in the night. If it's because of alcohol, stop or reduce drinking. If it's because of a bathroom urge, limit water intake after 7 or 8pm. Now, what if it's because of high stress?

Another two strategies:

- The worst-case-scenario bedtime page. If your learner is waking up with worry in the middle of the night—a small worry, like about a paper or test, not a big existential worry, nor a panic attack, both of which would benefit from tailored mental health support. If it's a lower-case w worry, then you can have them keep a sheet of paper by their bed for them to note their worry. It can be very simple. On the left-hand side of the page, they write their worry down. Maybe it's, "I'm worried I'll do badly on the Calculus test on Friday." On the right-hand side of the page, the learner can jot down in point form what steps they could take the next day to tend to that worry. Like a best-advice-to-self, like a small directive for the next day. A self-suggestion to ease the mind. It could, back to this example, be "practice 10 extra questions each day, especially on chapter 2." It takes you out of worry and into a plan; just having a worry without any next steps can be so punishing, *especially* in the wee hours of the morning.
- Next is rest. If our bodies go through the day without any breaks, without those brief, restful pauses, we might

be so tense or wound up that we can't relax enough to sleep. Incorporating moments of interest throughout the day—like taking short stretch breaks, resting with our legs up for a few minutes, deep breathing, practicing mindfulness, going for a walk around the block, playing with a pet, or sharing a laugh or hug with a friend—helps break up our busy days and improves our chances of achieving deep sleep.

It's interesting that the thing that's so essential—sleep—is often so elusive and challenging. Sometimes I wonder if it should actually be *the* most important "project" we work on. What if we gave even a fraction of our energy, time, and consideration to rest and sleep—how would we feel *and* how would our work go?

What I'm so keen for us to language to learners is that every cognitive function is enhanced with sleep. We're better at everything when we're rested. Focusing, thinking, listening, making connections, problem-solving, remembering, recalling.

In my 1:1 learning coaching with students, one of the first things we work on is sleep. Why? Because when a learner is rested, they can make it to their first class. And when you make it to the first class, making it to the second one is easier. (When you skip the first one, it can be hard to show up for the next one. And when you miss a class, it's easier to miss the next one, knowing you won't totally understand what's going on.)

There's a positive cascade when a learner is rested: attendance, and with attendance comes increased comprehension, and with increased comprehension comes improved focus, confidence, and performance.

And yet, the most common image of a student is that they're up late at night working away or studying. (Now, can a learner *just* sleep and *not* do their homework, complete assignments, or study? Nope. But all those things are not just easier but *likelier* when a student is well-rested.)

Sometimes, there's even a camaraderie or pride about just how late a learner stayed up to do their work. But as a family, as a micro-community, I hope you'll do it a little differently.

Raising a rested learner

And, you know, it's not just sleep. There are so many health-promoting activities that benefit our total well-being, quality of life, and even longevity, *and* that directly bolster academic performance as well. Nutrition, hydration, time in nature, community connection, and experiences of fun and play, these are all supportive to scholastic excellence—I long for these to take centre stage!

I feel like the big praise we can give our learners is not just that they got their work done, but that they did it *and* feel well, during and after. *That's* what I want to start languaging with learners. Praising the right thing. That they're taking care of themselves. That they have a sense of proportion. That they respect, love, and want to nurture their bodies. That they start their work early, practise a little-and-often, chipping away approach such that their work gets done to meet a deadline, and that, maybe, they've had a good night's sleep.

As parents and chosen family members, as mentors and educators, whether formal or informal, we can help the learners in our lives understand what's *truly* essential for school *and* holistic health—and that what's good for our health is good for academic performance!

Trusting the A Will Come

We worry about our kids constantly. In every which way.

A major worry is about how they're doing in school.

Are they listening? Are they understanding? Do they have friends? Are they "behaved" in class? Do they know that they can ask for help? Are they trying their best? Are they using the feedback they're given? Are they aware of their strengths and gifts? Are they hard on themselves? Are they paying attention? Are they overwhelmed, panicked, stressed, *dis*tresed?

Are they getting good grades?

This one is huge. It's not just learners who hold their breath when the report card comes home or the semester's transcript is ready. It's that moment of, (sharp inhale) "how did I do?" (no exhale). And the truth is, it's the same for us parents. We worry about how they're doing just as much.

The truly stunning thing is that students no longer have to wonder or worry quite as much—and nor do we. Assessment marks and final grades won't land as so surprising anymore.

How so?

In all of these chapters, all of these "hows" have been laid out. How to do school in all kinds of humane, health-promoting, holistic ways. It's not about doing all of them. But through nudging, emphasising, trying some right alongside your learner, shift will come. Maybe you're noticing them already?

It doesn't take many private sessions with student-clients for parents to write to me with effusive gratitude and feedback. I'm always touched, but also always reminded that it's entirely the student who's doing the work and the parents who are supporting it. I feel very clear that my role is to facilitate, guide, suggest, and coach; the credit is not mine. I will celebrate from the sidelines loudly, but I won't take what's not mine.

When students so bravely open up to new ways of thinking about and doing school, remarkable and *transformative* things happen.

Like what?

Here's the direct feedback I get from parents:

- They're happier at school.
- They get to school on time.
- They haven't missed a single class this semester.
- They're more rested.
- They're less snippy.
- They're getting their work done.
- They're not procrastinating anymore.
- They're not getting sick as often.
- They have more friends.
- They got involved in a school activity.
- They're on the Dean's list.
- They got into grad school.

- They got a scholarship.
- They got their first A.

Of course they did!

School success is mysteriously kept from students and families. Like students are either "good" at school, or they're not. But, I hope you and your learner really feel it in your bones that this is a flawed way of thinking. And that no matter the teacher, class, program, school, your learner can do well. So well. And *feel* well too.

That attendance streak, that new community of friends, that joy about class, that A—they're all by-products. They're, in a way, *inevitable*.

A's don't just happen. They're not "given." They're not accidental, they're not the be all and end all. They're just information and only one aspect of lots of different forms of feedback. They don't need to be the focus of a student's school journey, even if post-secondary or graduate school are the goal.

Marks, even if flawed, are just the ripple effect *of* well learning. When we're rested and focused, clear in instructions and planful with our time, experiencing a sense of welcome and belonging, co-regulated and confidently equipped with ways to move towards our heartfelt aims, the marks will come.

I'm not saying it's easy. I'm not saying it's not full of all kinds of ups and downs. I'm certainly not saying there aren't profound injustices in grading, and in assessment creation, and in curriculum and pedagogy—my life is devoted to making change with these. But for your family, for your learner, in the things you *can* do, those marks can be likelier to come.

How so?

It's in all of these outputs. It's in all of these well-being, whole person, deeply honouring practices along the way. Bit by bit. Little by little. Then, through the restedness and efficiencies and connections built and sense of self nourished, that A will come.

It's a leap of faith for some, I know. Especially for those learners and families who are in push-push-push mode. I'm in that mode a lot and was raised in that mode. But I also *know* it can be and feel so much different.

That A can come not just through sheer will, tight grips, clenched teeth, or working til' you drop; it can come with bringing a fulsome awakeness to when comprehension is shaky. It can come from the feedback that's given that we can lean into and grow from, by taking care of our bodies and spirits, and prioritising connection to our families, communities and the natural world.

Over time, by implementing the strategies throughout *Raising Well Learners*, I hope you and your learner can trust that the A *will* come.

About the Author

Dr. Deena Kara Shaffer has one question that continues to shape and fill her days: how can I help learners who are having a tough go of things? This has led Deena to a PhD in transformative learning strategies, serve as a high school teacher for students struggling with learning disabilities and addictions, become a post-secondary learning specialist, and thrive as a university lecturer on holistic education. Deena is Founder and CEO of Awakened Learning, offering 1:1 and group learning strategy coaching for students and parents, is a TEDx and keynote speaker on well-learning. Deena is the Director of the Office of Student and Academic Services at York University's Faculty of Environmental and Urban Change; and, the co-founder of Thriving in Action at Toronto Metropolitan University (Ryerson).

A national thought leader on humane teaching and learning, and author of the best-selling book, friend, and guide to students, "Feel Good Learning: On how to prioritise, focus, study and learn everything better," Deena offers a justice-focused, health-promoting approach to every educational encounter, including this exciting new project with Pandamonium Publishing House, to help parents help their kids through any age or stage of their learning journey.

Acknowledgements

A lifetime of thank yous.

To my students—Awakened Learning, SSH102, TiA, TMU, ASV, SOLA, Danforth Tech, Subway II.

To my colleagues—YorkU,TMU, LSAC, OCAD.

To my team—Vlada, Mona, Jenny, Nikki, Nicole, Mina, Kris, Nidhi.

To my champions—Hamza, Gina, Camille, Michelle, Avery, Ari, Alyssa, Chelsea, Mary Z, Dana, Hailey.

To my chosen fam—Meg, Agata, Jill, Yash, THE Menicuccis.

To my cherished three—Evelyn, Sasha, and Blaire.

To my missed two—my father, Ivan, and my mother, Anita.

To my beloved one—Andrew.

Thank you for each teaching me a part of this book, for revealing to me the point of my life, and for nudging me on to keep going. May the few minutes of my life make another's few minutes a little lighter.